Digital Photography

TOP 100 Simplified®

Tips & Tricks

From
maranGraphics®

&

Wiley Publishing, Inc.

Visual

Digital Photography: Top 100 Simplified® Tips & Tricks

Published by
Wiley Publishing, Inc.
111 River Street
Hoboken, NJ 07030

Published simultaneously in Canada

Copyright © 2003 by Wiley Publishing, Inc., Indianapolis, Indiana

Certain designs, text, and illustrations Copyright © 1992-2003 maranGraphics, Inc., used with maranGraphics permission.

maranGraphics, Inc.
5755 Coopers Avenue
Mississauga, Ontario, Canada
L4Z 1R9

Library of Congress Control Number: 2003110440

ISBN: 0-7645-4447-0

Manufactured in the United States of America

10 9 8 7 6 5 4 3

1K/RT/QY/QT/IN

Trademark Acknowledgments

Important Numbers

For U.S. corporate orders, please call maranGraphics at 800-469-6616 or fax 905-890-9434.

For general information on our other products and services or to obtain technical support please contact our Customer Care Department within the U.S. at 800-762-2974, outside the U.S. at 317-572-3993 or fax 317-572-4002.

Permissions

Wiley Publishing, Inc.

is a trademark of Wiley Publishing, Inc.

U.S. Corporate Sales
Contact maranGraphics at (800) 469-6616 or fax (905) 890-9434.

U.S. Trade Sales
Contact Wiley at (800) 762-2974 or fax (317) 572-4002.

CREDITS

Project Editor:
Timothy J. Borek

Acquisitions Editor:
Michael Roney

Product Development Manager:
Lindsay Sandman

Copy Editor:
Jill Mazurczyk

Technical Editor:
Dennis Short

Editorial Manager:
Rev Mengle

Permissions Editor:
Laura Moss

Editorial Assistant
Adrienne Porter

Manufacturing:
Allan Conley
Linda Cook
Paul Gilchrist
Jennifer Guynn

Special Help:
Tom Heine
Sherry Kinkopn
Jody Lefevere
Rev Mengle
Adrienne Porter
Maureen Spears

Book Design:
maranGraphics, Inc.

Production Coordinator:
Nancee Reeves

Layout:
LeAndra Hosier
Kristin McMullan
Kathie S. Schnorr

Screen Artist:
Jill A. Proll

Illustrators:
Ronda David-Burroughs
David E. Gregory

Proofreader:
Laura L. Bowman

Quality Control:
Laura Albert
John Tyler Connoley

Indexer:
Sherry Massey

Vice President and Executive Group Publisher:
Richard Swadley

Vice President and Publisher:
Barry Pruett

Composition Director:
Debbie Stailey

maranGraphics is a family-run business
located near Toronto, Canada.

At **maranGraphics**, we believe in producing great computer books—one book at a time.

Each maranGraphics book uses the award-winning communication process that we have been developing over the last 28 years. Using this process, we organize screen shots and text in a way that makes it easy for you to learn new concepts and tasks.

We spend hours deciding the best way to perform each task, so you don't have to! Our clear, easy-to-follow screen shots and instructions walk you through each task from beginning to end.

We want to thank you for purchasing what we feel are the best computer books money can buy. We hope you enjoy using this book as much as we enjoyed creating it!

Sincerely,

The Maran Family

HOW TO USE THIS BOOK

**Digital Photography: Top 100 Simplified®
Tips & Tricks** includes the 100 most interesting
and useful tasks you can perform with a digital
camera. This book reveals cool secrets and
timesaving tricks guaranteed to make you more
productive in using image-editing software.

Who is this book for?

Are you a visual learner who already knows
the basics of digital photography, but would
like to take your digital photography
experience to the next level? Then this is
the book for you.

Conventions In This Book

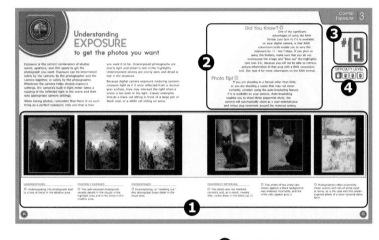

① Steps

This book walks you through each task
using a step-by-step approach. Lines and
"lassos" connect the screen shots to the
step-by-step instructions to show you
exactly how to perform each task.

② Tips

Fun and practical tips answer questions
you have always wondered about. Plus,
learn to do things with digital
photography that you never through
were possible!

③ Task Numbers

The task numbers, ranging from 1 to 100,
indicate which self-contained lesson you
are currently working on.

④ Difficulty Levels

For quick reference, symbols mark the
difficulty level of each task.

Demonstrates a new spin on
a common task

Introduces a new skill or a
new task

Combines multiple skills
requiring in-depth knowledge

Requires extensive skill and
may involve other technologies

TABLE OF CONTENTS

Get Ready to Take Photos

Take Better Photos

Control Exposure

Control Focus and Depth of Field

TABLE OF CONTENTS

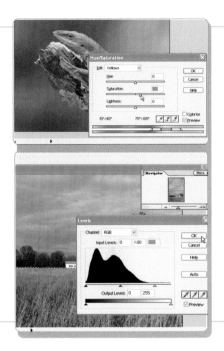
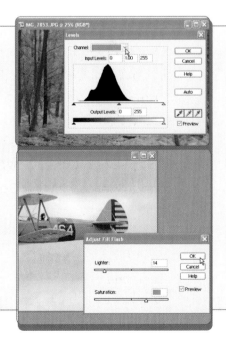

TABLE OF **CONTENTS**

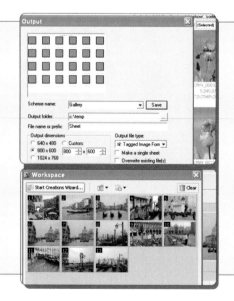

CHAPTER 1

Get Ready to Take Photos

Whether you are a snapshot photographer recording people, places, and events that are meaningful to you, or you are a passionate photographer who gets immense joy from taking photographs for yourself or others, you can improve your photography if you do the right things before you shoot.

Choosing what and where to shoot is the first step you must take before shooting. Learn to find good events, places, and subjects to shoot by reading newspapers, books, or online resources. Look for good photo opportunities at local fairs, botanical gardens, nature preserves, national parks, or even zoos. Consider shooting still life or setting up a studio inside where you can control lighting.

When you know what you will be shooting, make sure you know all that you can know about your digital camera. The more you know about your equipment, the more you can concentrate on taking photographs as you want them and not on learning how to use your camera. It can be very disappointing spending valuable time and money to take a trip only to find that you did not take good photos due to improper camera settings or usage.

When you go to shoot, be realistic; a day of shooting will not always result in one or more good photos. All photographers have bad days where they end up with no good photos — especially when the shooting conditions work against you!

TOP 100

Select good PHOTO OPPORTUNITIES

Unless you have specific reasons to shoot particular scenes or subjects, the best photo opportunities for you are of those things that you enjoy. If you enjoy gardening and appreciate the thousands of different variations of iris, then shoot irises. If you are a birdwatcher or find pleasure in watching wildlife, choose places where you can find birds and other wildlife in settings that make great photographs.

When planning a trip, give yourself plenty of time to stay and take photographs. Allow yourself some time for bad weather or other shooting conditions that prevent you from photographing. You can spend an entire day or more at a site and not have good enough light to shoot. Do not fall into the trap of trying to see too much too quickly. You may miss the kinds of shots you had hoped to capture because you saw everything and shot little. Photography takes time, and time is often the most important factor in getting truly great photographs.

O Waiting just a few minutes allowed the gondola to be shown in this photo of the Grand Canal in Venice.

O It took several hours of waiting to get a shadow on this otherwise overly bright photograph of the White House ruins in Canyon de Chelly in Arizona.

O If you are willing to hike, you may be rewarded with photos that are well worth the effort it took to get there.

Photo Tip! ☀

When you find a good place to take photographs, visit it again and again. Your photographs will improve each time you revisit a location, because you will learn when to visit and what to shoot.

Did You Know? ☀

Some of the best photo opportunities may be in your own backyard. Learn to see differently and look for details, shapes, or colors that make good photographs, and then capture them.

Photo Tip! ☀

Use the Internet to learn where and when to shoot. Many online guides and forums provide all the information you need to find wonderful places and subjects to shoot that will suit your interests.

O This small backyard pond offers many subjects to photograph. Being close to home, it is easy to shoot in the best light.

O This frog is sunning on a rock on the edge of the pond shown in the photo to the left.

KNOW WHY
you are taking photos

Should you shoot horizontally or vertically? If you have a choice of digital cameras, which one should you use? What camera settings will you use? Will your photographs be framed or displayed on a Web page? Are you going to include your photographs in a series or should they be shot in a particular style? Are you shooting to get backgrounds or objects to include in another photograph? Do you plan on digitally editing your photographs with an image editor like Adobe Photoshop Elements after you take them?

Your answers to these questions and others like them will have a substantial impact on how you should shoot. Knowing why you are taking photos before you take them can help you get the photos that you want. For example, suppose you make a once-in-a-lifetime trip and get excellent pictures. You then decide to make a calendar, but cannot find enough photos to fit the horizontal format you have chosen. Thinking about why you are taking the photographs and how they are likely to be viewed can help you to better plan your photographs.

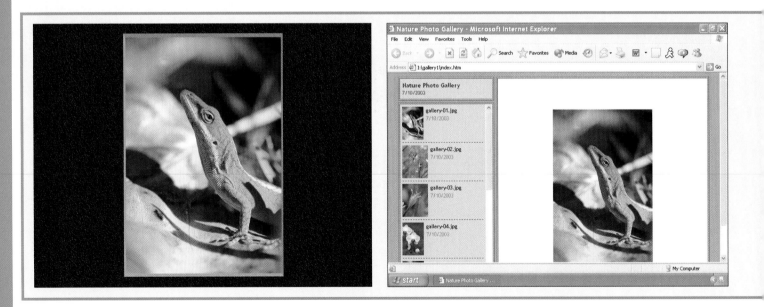

O This photo of a green anole was taken so that it could be used in a variety of media.

O Minor cropping allows the photo to display in a Web browser-based photo gallery.

Photo Tip! ☀

When you know that you will share a photo online, you can take advantage of the "multiplication factor" that you get when you crop an image from a large image. A small bird in a mostly blue sky photo can become a large bird that fills the frame when it is cropped.

Did You Know? ☀

Custom-sized frames and matte boards can be considerably more expensive than those of standard sizes. When possible, you should consider shooting so that you can use standard 3" x 5", 5" x 7", 8" x 10", and 10" x 13" frames and matte boards.

Did You Know? ☀

A good photograph for the cover of a magazine usually needs to be shot vertically with some space on the photo where text and graphics may be placed without interfering with the composition of the subject.

O Vertical orientation and composition makes it possible to frame this photo in standard-sized photo frames and matte boards.

O Good cover design allowed the leaf on the left side of the photo to be used for the magazine's cover text.

MASTER YOUR CAMERA
to get great photos

Today's sophisticated digital cameras allow anyone to take good, and sometimes great, photographs by simply using one of the automatic shooting modes and pressing the shutter release. However, most digital cameras offer many additional features that give serious photographers considerable creative control over how photos are taken and ensure that a higher percentage of photos are taken as desired.

One major advantage of most digital cameras is that you may review the image and the camera settings on an LCD screen immediately after taking a photo.

This allows you to check that you have composed the photo as you wanted and that the camera settings were set as you expected. Some digital cameras even provide a *histogram* to give you a graphical view of the exposure. These review features are well worth using.

To get the best photos, learn all that you can about your digital camera. You must master your camera or it will limit your success.

O This dial on a Canon PowerShot G2 controls the shooting modes.

O The Canon PowerShot G2 LED screen shows important camera settings at a glance.

Did You Know? ※

The more you learn about and use different features on your camera, the easier it becomes to forget which settings you have changed and to shoot using the wrong settings. Learn how to quickly check your settings or to set them to the default settings in order to avoid shooting with the wrong settings. Many photos are ruined because of improper camera settings. The most common camera settings that can ruin photos are exposure compensation, white balance, auto-ISO change, and image size.

Warning! ※

Many digital cameras have shooting modes that automatically choose a faster ISO setting if there is not sufficient light. Make sure you know which shooting modes allow this to avoid taking photos that have too much digital noise.

O Important camera settings are controlled on the Canon PowerShot G2 via multiple menus.

O The LCD screen on the Canon PowerShot G2 shows a screen with camera settings, a histogram, and a thumbnail image.

Choose the
IMAGE FILE FORMAT
to suit your needs

Each time you press the shutter release, you capture an image on the image sensor. The image is then written to a file in a user-selected format with or without your chosen camera settings being applied. Most digital cameras offer three formats: JPEG (.jpg), TIFF (.tif), and RAW format.

The most commonly used format is the JPEG format. It offers a good balance between image file size and image quality. The JPEG format is a *lossy* format, meaning that it uses a mathematical algorithm to reduce the file size while losing some image quality.

The TIFF format is a *nonlossy* format, which means that no image quality is lost, but files are considerably larger.

Unlike JPEG and TIFF files, RAW image files are proprietary files that do not have most of the camera settings applied to them. For greater creative flexibility, the photographer can use a RAW image converter, such as the Adobe Camera RAW Plug-in (see task #61 and task #62), and apply camera settings to the file *after* the photo has been taken.

Approximate Image File Sizes

Image Size	TIFF	JPEG	RAW
5-Megapixel Image	14.5MB	1.5MB	7.8MB
Compression Ratio	1:1	10:1	2:1

○ RAW format images are digital "negatives" that need to be digitally processed to be viewed and edited.

○ These file sizes are from a Nikon Coolpix 5700. File sizes from other digital cameras will vary.

DIFFICULTY LEVEL

Did You Know? ※

RAW image files are the best image format to use if you want to get the best possible pictures from your digital camera. Camera settings such as white balance, color correction, levels, sharpening, and other settings are not applied to a RAW image file. After you shoot, you have control over these settings when processing them with a RAW image converter such as the Adobe Camera RAW Plug-in (see task #61 and task #62) or one provided by your camera manufacturer. Many serious photographers shoot in RAW format most of the time.

Did You Know? ※

RAW image file converters enable you to add exposure compensation to your photos after you have taken them by up to or more than plus or minus two f-stops! That alone makes it worthwhile to shoot in RAW format.

| Advantages of JPEG Over RAW File Format ||
JPEG	*RAW*
- All camera settings are applied	+ Few camera settings are applied
+ Smaller file size	- Larger file size
+ Easily viewable images	- Requires proprietary conversion software
+ Quick to view	- Slower to view
- 8-bit image	+ Wider-bit range (10 or 12-bits)

Set IMAGE RESOLUTION
and compression level

In addition to letting you choose a file format for your photos, most digital cameras also enable you to choose image resolution. If you have chosen the JPEG file format, many cameras also let you specify the compression level. Image resolution is expressed in terms of pixels such as 2,560 x 1,920 pixels. If you multiply these two numbers together you get the total pixel count. 2,560 x 1,920 = 4,915,200, or just about 5 megapixels. More pixels in a picture enable you to print a larger print, which is the primary reason to buy a more expensive digital camera with a higher megapixel rating.

There is a tradeoff between the number of pixels and the image file size — the more pixels, the larger the file. To fit more digital photos on digital photo storage media, the JPEG file format allows you to select the level of compression, which reduces file size. Unfortunately, the more an image is compressed, the lower the image quality. To choose the optimal settings for your photography, you need to balance the tradeoffs between image size (resolution), compression level, image quality, and possible print size.

O This photo was taken with a 3.1-megapixel camera with an image size of 2,160 x 1,440 pixels.

O This 800 x 600-pixel image was taken from the center of the image on the left. It makes an excellent full-size Web page photo.

Did You Know? ✺

By reducing image resolution to store more photos, you lose the benefits of image cropping and the ability to get a larger print later. As digital photo storage media prices continue to drop, you can buy one or more extra cards and use the maximum image resolution and the least image compression. This decision enables you to avoid getting a prized shot that is too small or has too much compression to make a good print.

Did You Know? ✺

Each time you save a JPEG file after editing it, your image degrades. Therefore, if you need to open, edit, and save a JPEG image more than once, you should save all but the final images in a non-compressed image format such as TIFF, bitmap (.bmp), or Photoshop (.psd).

Print Size		
Megapixels	*Image Resolution*	*Print Size*
2	1,200 x 1,600	5" x 6.7"
3	1,512 x 2,016	6.3" x 8.4"
4	1,704 x 2,272	7.1" x 9.5"
5	1,944 x 2,592	8.1" x 10.8"
6	2,048 x 3,072	8.5" x 12.8"

O Assumes optimal printing is 240 DPI.

Control camera's
LIGHT SENSITIVITY
with ISO setting

In traditional film photography, you choose film based upon an *ISO rating* (the new term for ASA setting), such as ISO 100 or ISO 400, depending on how much light you expect to have when you shoot. Photographers consider film with a low ISO rating, such as ISO 100, to be a slower film than ISO 400 because it takes a longer shutter speed to properly expose the film than film with a higher ISO rating, which enables an image to be recorded more quickly.

Digital cameras also enable you to change ISO settings between each shot. Choosing an ISO setting is one of the most important settings that you can make. Although a faster ISO setting such as ISO 400 or 800 lets you shoot in lower-light settings without image blur due to long exposure times, you will end up with considerably more digital noise in your digital photos. Digital noise is similar to grain in traditional photography and is generally an undesirable tradeoff you get when using higher ISO settings.

O This photo was shot at ISO 800 to enable a faster shutter speed to avoid image blur in the low light.

O Digital noise is easily visible in most of this photo.

#6

Did You Know? ☀

You generally get the best picture quality by using the lowest ISO setting your camera offers, such as ISO 50 or 100. A higher setting such as ISO 400 or 800 will have considerably more digital noise.

Did You Know? ☀

When you edit a digital photo with an image editor, such as Adobe Photoshop Elements, you are likely to get more pronounced digital noise when you perform steps such as increasing contrast, increasing image size, and sharpening an image.

Photo Tip! ☀

While digital noise is generally an unwanted characteristic of a digital photo, you can use it as a creative design element. The digital noise gives the photo a grainy effect similar to the grain found in traditional photographic prints.

DIFFICULTY LEVEL

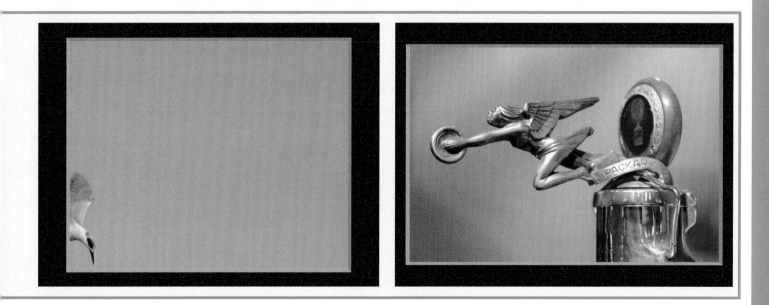

O No digital noise appears in this photo, which was shot at ISO 100.

O ISO 800 was used to achieve a traditional film grain effect in this black-and-white photo.

Improve color with
WHITE BALANCE
setting

One of the more significant challenges facing digital photographers is to take photographs with accurate color. A common problem is getting a photo that has a *color-cast,* which means that the photo has too much a certain color, such as blue, red, or yellow. An improper white balance setting often causes this problem. An in-camera white balance setting allows you to record correct colors when shooting under a variety of different lighting conditions such as incandescent light, tungsten light, sunshine, or clouds.

Besides letting users choose an appropriate white balance setting, many digital cameras have a custom white balance setting that can record very accurate colors after you first take a photo of a white card. If your camera offers such a feature, it is worth learning about and using. One of the surer ways to get accurate color is to shoot in RAW mode, which enables you to change the white balance setting using a RAW converter long after you take the photo. Most RAW converters, such as the Adobe RAW Camera Plug-in (see task #61 and task #62), have controls that can fine-tune the white balance.

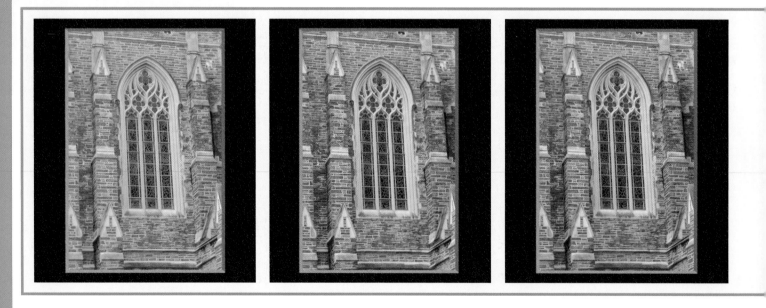

O This photo was taken outdoors on a cloudy day with white balance set incorrectly to tungsten.

O This photo was taken outdoors on a cloudy day with white balance set incorrectly to cloudy.

O This photo was taken outdoors on a cloudy day with the camera's white balance set to auto white balance.

Photo Tip! ☀

Sometimes you can add a
preset white balance setting to
add a desirable color tone to a photo.
For example, using a cloudy white
balance setting can add warmth to an
otherwise cold or blue-toned image.

Did You Know? ☀

Most digital image editors offer several color-
correction tools. However, many of them work
best if you have a pure white or neutral gray tone
in your image. When you are concerned about getting
accurate color, and you do not have a pure white or
neutral gray tone in the composition, consider placing
a white card in the photo. After you use the white
area for color correction purposes, you can remove
it with your digital image editor.

DIFFICULTY LEVEL

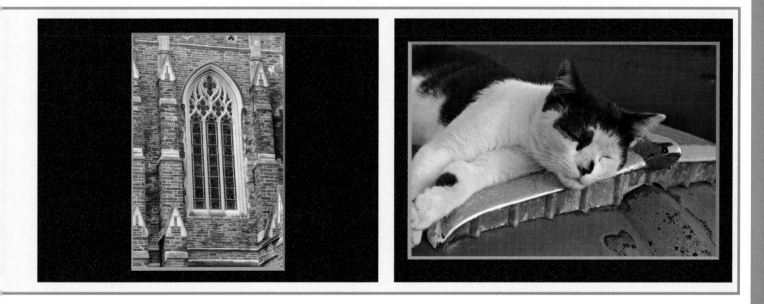

O This photo was taken outdoors on a
cloudy day using the RAW format, so
the camera's white balance setting is
not applied.

O While accurate color can mean
white is pure white, some of the
golden glow of sunset will bathe
the scene in a warm color.

Shoot for
DIGITAL EDITING

Taking a photograph with a digital camera is one small part — albeit a significant part — of the entire digital photography process. If you shoot digitally without considering the possibilities of what you can do later in an image editor, you will dramatically limit your creativity and your picture-making ability.

To take advantage of the new world of digital photography, you should become as familiar with an image editor like Adobe Photoshop Elements as you are with your camera. Learn how your image editor enables you to combine, fix, distort, correct, tint, or otherwise change your photos to become more than

they were. Digitally stitching multiple images together into a single panoramic photograph, increasing tonal range and image contrast, and creating photographs with a full dynamic range are just a few of the wonders you can achieve when you become proficient with an image editor.

Although a digital image editor provides you tremendous image-manipulation power, do not forget that you can always do more with well-taken photos that you can with marginally acceptable ones. Great image editing always begins with an excellent photograph.

○ This photo of tree bark was taken to use as a background for another photo.

○ This simple photo of a tree was taken to combine with a background photo.

○ This image was made by combining the two photos on the left.

○ Adobe Photoshop Elements filters and plug-ins were used to create this painted image of the tree shown on the left.

Photo Tip! ※

After you have purchased a digital camera and some digital photo storage media, taking photos does not cost anything, so shoot often — and then shoot again. Learn to try different exposure settings and compositions, and shoot plenty of shots so that you have a choice between several good ones.

Did You Know? ※

You can use an image editor like Adobe Photoshop Elements to remove or add photographic elements such as telephone lines, sky, clouds, people, and so on. If you have composed a photo that has a distracting element, shoot anyway and fix it later in your image editor. (See task #63.) Just remember that it is usually easier to shoot a photo that does not need correction in an image editor than it is to have to edit it later.

#8

DIFFICULTY LEVEL

○ A row of old trucks was transformed into this image with Adobe Photoshop Elements.

○ Five separate photos were combined to create this image of kids and seagulls flying over the coast.

PACK
for a successful and enjoyable shoot

Patiently waiting is often a key part of photography. Depending on your shooting conditions, you may have to wait for better light, less or more rain, for a subject to appear, for a cloud to move, or even for the sun to rise or set. In any event, patience can be the most important personality trait a photographer can have to get good photographs. The best way to strengthen that trait is to bring along items that will make your outing more enjoyable, productive, and safe.

If you are too hot or too cold, hungry, tired, or you are being bitten by bugs, you are likely to take fewer good photos than if you are a happy and comfortable photographer. Before you head off for a shoot, carefully consider what you should take with you in addition to your photography equipment. A few nutrition bars, water, a lightweight folding chair, sunscreen, and a hat can unquestionably contribute to your taking better photographs.

O A lightweight folding tripod chair makes it easy for this photographer to quietly wait for a bullfrog to pop his head above water.

O Water, a hat, sunscreen, insect repellent, and snacks are just a few things that will make your picture-taking time more enjoyable.

Did You Know? ※

Some of the most useful information for photographers is found on the Internet.

Hiking equipment: www.rei.com

Online mapping service: www.mapquest.com

Weather: www.weather.com or www.weatherbug.com

Best state parks: http://usparks.about.com/blbestparks.htm

All-encompassing outdoor page: http://gorp.com/index.html

Sun and moon timetable:
http://aa.usno.navy.mil/data/docs/RS_OneDay.html

DIFFICULTY LEVEL

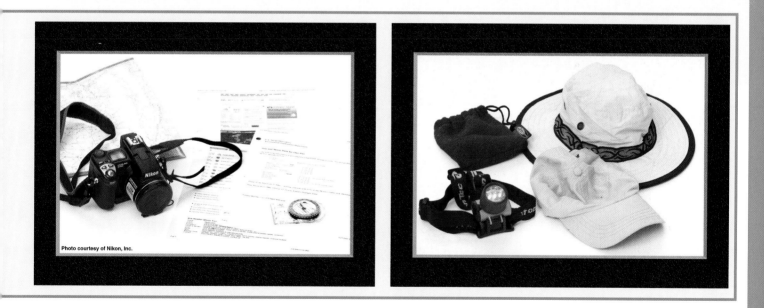

Photo courtesy of Nikon, Inc.

O A compass and a schedule of the sunrise and sunset will make it easier for you to be in the right place at the right time to get the best of the sunlight.

O Use a headlamp like the Princeton-Tec to make your walks safe when hiking to capture early morning or late-evening light.

CHAPTER 2

Take Better Photos

Taking good photographs has more to do with a photographer's vision, the time she has to spend shooting, reviewing, and digitally editing her photos, and the knowledge of her camera, than with buying and using expensive photographic equipment. Undoubtedly, some of the more expensive digital cameras enable you to take better photographs, but if you really want to improve your photographic success, learn how to shoot better. Learn to choose subjects that you are passionate about. Assess and choose good shooting conditions. Determine your own photographic vision, and use your knowledge of your camera to capture that vision.

You also need lots of time to shoot, study, edit, and wait. You may need to wait for better light, less wind, or even for your desired subjects to arrive. When conditions are good and you are ready to shoot, you must have your photographic vision and an understanding of how to compose. The exciting new world of digital photography offers every photographer many new benefits that make it easier, faster, and cheaper to learn to make excellent photographs more often.

What makes a good photo? One of the best standards to use to determine if you have taken a good photograph is simply asking yourself if you like it, and if you enjoyed the process of making it. Listen to the advice and opinions of others, but shoot for yourself and your own enjoyment. If you do, and you work hard and put in the time, you will become a good—maybe even a great—photographer.

TOP 100

Assess
SHOOTING CONDITIONS

You should make it a habit to carefully assess shooting conditions before taking any pictures, for many reasons. Besides determining if shooting is worth your time to at all, you should decide how to get the best photographs you can from the existing conditions. You may also consider when you might want to return to get better photographs.

What are good shooting conditions? Does wind, rain, snow, or bright midday sun make conditions bad for shooting? One of the amazing things about photography is that there are few rules that *always* hold true. While it is safe to say that getting good photos is more difficult with midday sun, you can find many remarkable examples of how wrong always accepting such a guideline as a rule is.

Also, consider the subject as one of your most important shooting conditions. If you are passionate about the subject, you will not only enjoy shooting more, but your results ultimately will be better. Having an interest in and some knowledge about the subject can help you capture and portray the soul of the subject in an exciting or interesting way.

○ Would an early morning shot with light illuminating the white farm buildings improve this evening shot?

○ Is this a good beach color? Will it get better later? Should a faster shutter speed be used to underexpose it a bit for richer colors?

○ Might a better background be chosen for this white poodle?

#10

Photo Tip! ※

When you are shooting in less
than ideal conditions, look for
inventive ways to get good photos. A
torrential downpour may leave you with
wonderful patterns in water puddles that
reflect your subject. Or, wind that is too fast to
allow you to take close-up photos may help you to
get award-winning soft-focus photos if you use a slow
shutter speed to capture blowing flowers.

Did You Know? ※

A surprising number of excellent photographs
have been taken in what is known as "bad"
weather. Heavy fog, thunderstorms, and snow
blizzards often make for excellent photographs. The
next time you think the weather is bad, go shoot and
see what you get. Look for low-contrast shooting
conditions, lightning or "edges" between a storm with
dramatic lighting and a calm area.

○ Is there too much wind to get a well-
focused photo of this bee bathed in rich
garden colors? Or, might the wind help to
create a soft-focus effect?

○ Can good photos be taken in a
snowstorm? How will this scene look in
an hour, or two hours, or even more?

Consider the
POSSIBILITIES

Each time you press the shutter button to take a picture, you analyze dozens of different variables, including exposure, composition, lighting, depth of field, angle of view, and ISO setting. To get better photos, think about how you can change the variables to take many different photographs. Study the results to find the ones you like.

The more you experiment and study your results, the more you understand what you like and how to further develop your own personal style. For good practice, carefully consider how you can shoot differently. Because many good photographers shoot the same subjects, getting fresh and interesting photographs that you will be proud of demands considerable thought.

When one of the world's most famous photographers was asked to review another photographer's portfolio, he looked quickly and said, "Take a couple of weeks and go shoot a few thousand more photos." He made that comment because the photographer had not yet considered enough of the possibilities.

○ Exposure was increased slightly over metered exposure to brighten the statue.

○ This exposure was the result of the camera's metering.

○ A slightly underexposed setting causes the background to disappear.

○ This slightly tighter framed photo puts more attention on the hand gesture.

Apply It!

You can sometimes get new and interesting photographs by going to extremes. Shoot using extreme f-stops, extreme shutter speeds, and extreme angles of views. Then, back off just a bit. Maybe try the other extreme and then back off just a bit. Ample experimentation will eventually yield photos you like.

 # 11

DIFFICULTY LEVEL

Did You Know?

The most common view of a subject or a scene is from a vantage point about five to six feet from the ground. Because most people view the world from this height, photos taken from this height are often ordinary. Try shooting from a worm's-eye or bird's-eye view to give viewers a fresh or unusual perspective.

O This tightly cropped photo emphasizes the face.

O This horizontal composition helps the viewer feel more "face to face" with the statue.

COMPOSE
for maximum effect

How you compose is one of the most important decisions that you make about any photograph that you take. Although many guidelines help you to compose well, most of them have been routinely broken while still resulting in outstanding photographs. So, use the common rules such as the "rule of thirds" as a mere guideline, not a hard and fast rule that cannot be broken.

Using a digital camera with a zoom lens enables you to try different compositions without having to move as much. You can shoot a wide-angle photo and then zoom in to compose a much tighter view of the subject. Angle-of-view and vantage points are two other significant aspects of composition that you can control somewhat when using a zoom lens. Look for creative angles that show your subject or scene in new and interesting ways. Also, look for ways to accentuate form, texture, and patterns. If you have composed a photo that invites the viewer to look more closely, most likely you have composed well.

O This photo was composed by the "rule of thirds," where the main subject is located on one of the intersecting lines of an imaginary tic-tac-toe board overlaid on the image.

O Framing the swamp with the foreground trees made this more interesting than an unframed version.

O Adding a long expanse of the rusty hood in this photo helps to explain where this dirty junkyard cat is napping in the sun.

Apply It! ※

You can help convey information to the viewer about the subject by framing a photo with the foreground. Applying this powerful technique also makes viewers feel like they are in the scene. Without this foreground, there is nothing but the subject.

DIFFICULTY LEVEL

Did You Know? ※

It takes effort to see new ways to compose. Yet, if you took a dozen good photographers and asked them to shoot the same subject, there would be many, many different compositions. Find a subject and see how many different compositions you can shoot as an exercise to further your composition skills.

○ A soft background keeps focus on the two drink glasses and makes the viewer wonder about who might be drinking them.

○ This very graphic architecture is further made into a graphic by composing the shot at an angle.

Shoot photos based on a
THEME

For a number of good reasons, you should try to shoot photos based on a theme. First, if you have chosen a theme that you have interest in, you will enjoy taking the photographs for it and it can be a motivating factor to get you shooting. You will also find that you will become a better photographer as you continue to learn and work toward getting better and better photographs of a similar subject. Having more than one or just a few photos of a subject helps you to compare what is good and not so good in each shot you take.

You can choose to shoot a theme that can be completed; for example, all the country churches in a specific county. Or, you can choose a more open-ended theme such as antique automobiles, old barns, or even gargoyles. The photos below are a good example of one very specific theme. All the photos are of antique automobile hood ornaments. Notice all but one of them are Mack truck hood ornaments. What theme should you pick?

O This Mack truck hood ornament was shot to have a soft background.

O This is a hood ornament from a Mack fire truck.

O The rust on this hood ornament gives a clue to the age of the vehicle it is mounted on.

DIFFICULTY LEVEL

Apply It! ※

As you shoot photos based on a theme, carefully consider how you compose them and how they will work together as a series. Should you shoot some in portrait mode and others in landscape mode? Should you attempt to have similar backgrounds or can the backgrounds vary?

Did You Know? ※

If you have chosen a theme that requires considerable searching, use the Internet to get help shooting your theme. If you are a bird photographer, find a forum where other birders can tell you where to find certain birds. Or, maybe you need help finding old barns. The Internet can save you considerable time and travel expense when searching for subjects that fit your theme.

O This graceful hood ornament is from an antique Packard automobile.

O Another Mack truck hood ornament shown against a rusted truck body.

Work to
DEVELOP
YOUR STYLE

If you have seen a photograph and said, "That photograph had to have been taken by . . ." and then correctly named the photographer, you have found a photographer who has a well-developed *style*. What makes a style? It can be the way a photographer portrays a subject, uses light, or captures colors. Or it may be a more difficult-to-quantify combination of characteristics that, when combined, make the style noteworthy.

How do you develop a style of your own? Take lots of photographs to develop your photographic vision and learn more about what it is you see and how you portray it. After you have taken thousands of photos, you will begin to see a pattern. Maybe you have an eye for shooting things that are graphic with bold colors, or you have worked on an impressionistic style by shooting in soft light on windy days with slow shutter speeds. When you notice a style developing, work on it to make it more distinctive, and keep refining it.

O This purple and yellow iris is isolated from the soft green background with a telephoto lens.

O The vantage point was chosen to provide a sharp contrast between the purple iris and the soft green background.

O Aperture was chosen to keep this iris entirely in focus while allowing the background to be soft.

O The distance from the iris to the background helped make a soft background for this sharply focused iris.

#14

DIFFICULTY LEVEL

Did You Know? ☀

Many of the world's most successful and well-known photographers have a style that makes their work notable. Check out the works of Annie Leibowitz, Freeman Patterson, Pete Turner, and Jerry Uelsmann to name just a few of the more noteable ones with easily recognized styles.

Did You Know? ☀

If you want to sell your photographs in most art shows or display them in galleries, you are more likely to have your work shown if you have a distinct style, shoot on a theme, or both. A series of random photographs with no connection can be considerably less interesting than a group of photos with a consistent style or theme.

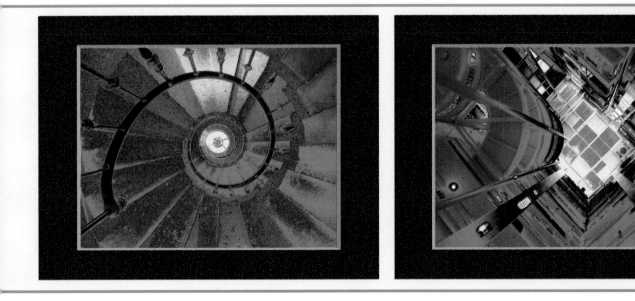

O These two photos taken by Larry Berman (www.alternatephoto.com) show a style unique to Larry because of the color infrared technique he uses and the way he portrays ordinary subjects.

O Part of Larry Berman's style involves choosing ordinary subjects but shooting them in extraordinary ways.

SHOOT DETAILS
to create interest

While the first and natural inclination is to shoot an entire subject, shooting tightly cropped details can lead to the creation of captivating photos. Detail photos often are more interesting than full-subject shots because you can take a photograph that either shows detail the viewer had never noticed or detail that may cause a viewer to take a closer look while wondering what the subject is.

Capturing just part of a subject enables you to put emphasis on the detail that is ordinarily overlooked when viewing the entire subject. When composing detail photos, compose to show form, color, texture, or shape.

When shooting details, be aware of the fact that you can shoot an increasing level of detail too. For example, you can shoot just part of a tree with an interesting shape, such as a specific branch, a few leaves, a single leaf, or even just part of a leaf showing the intricate lines and texture. As you get to increasingly smaller detail, you may want to consider using a macro lens or macro feature.

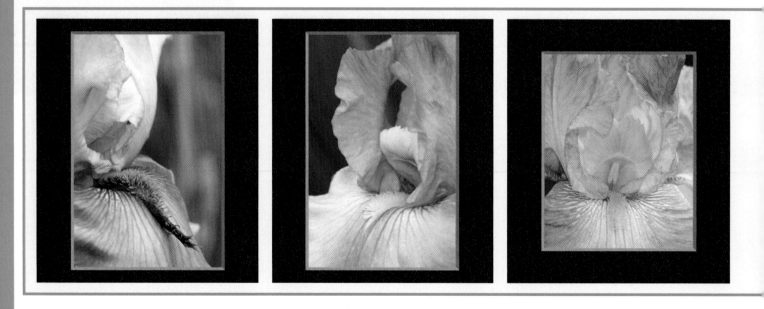

O Close-up photos of these irises were taken to reveal details not ordinarily noticed in photographs that show the entire iris.

O The graceful, flowing shape of the beard of an iris is shown by this close-up photo.

O This straight-on photo shows the intricate details of an iris.

Apply It! ☀

To catch a viewer's interest,
take a photo of just part of a
subject to let the viewer imagine what
the rest of the subject looks like or to
even make them wonder what it is that they
are looking at. Also, detail-oriented photos can
frequently reveal details to viewers that they would
not normally have noticed.

Photo Tip ☀

When shooting a detailed photo with a small
subject, use a macro lens or shoot in macro
mode if one is available on your digital camera.
Shooting with a shallow depth-of-field can often
further add to the success of the photo.

#15

DIFFICULTY LEVEL

○ Detail photo of the arched concrete
support beams in a church walkway that
connects two buildings.

○ Details of just part of this ornate
chapel wall make an interesting photo.

Compose for final
PRINT
PROPORTIONS

One challenge when photographing with a digital camera is to compose an image in the viewfinder that will translate into a printed image with the width-to-height proportions that you want. This problem arises because the ratio of the image sensor is usually not the same ratio as the paper you print on or the proportions of the image you want to put on a Web page.

Even though your images may be composed perfectly in the viewfinder, the viewfinder does not have the same proportions as many standard-sized prints, such as 8" x 10" or 4" x 6". This means you have to crop the printed image. Think about how you will use your photos and shoot accordingly. To avoid having a less than perfect photo for any purpose, shoot more than one photo composed for each intended use. The owl photos below show how hard it was to get even one standard-sized print that looked good from the original photo that fills the frame. Most of these photos look too "tight" and the cropping removes some of the wonderful glowing background colors.

O This original uncropped image fits well within the camera's viewfinder.

O More space above the owl's head would be nice in this 11" x 14" print.

O More space above the owl's head would be nice in this 8" x 10" print.

#16

Caution! ※

If you are concerned about having to crop an image to get the width-to-height proportions for a print (such as a 5" x 7" or 8" x 10") or an image for a Web page (640 pixels by 480 pixels), make sure you have set your camera to the largest resolution setting and compose to show a smaller subject. If you use less than the maximum resolution, you may not have an image that is suitable for your intended use after it has been cropped, as cropping may reduce the image size below what is needed.

Did You Know? ※

Using a digital image editor like Adobe Photoshop Elements, you can add some width or height to a photo if you are unable to crop it to the width-to-height proportions you want. After adding some width or height to your image, use a cloning tool to paint in some needed width or height.

○ The owl is too tightly cropped all around in this 5" x 7" print.

○ This 4" x 6" print works well, unlike all the other standard sizes, as the background shows over the head of the owl and to the right of the owl, where it is looking.

○ This 10" x 8" print shows the difficulty of composing horizontally when a shot is taken vertically.

Shoot better using
EXIF DATA

When you take a digital picture, the camera writes the image to an image file along with other useful additional information such as the date and time the picture was taken. The camera also records settings such as shutter speed, aperture, exposure compensation, program mode, ISO speed, metering mode, white balance setting, flash information, and others.

All this information is written to the image file in an industry standard format called the *EXIF* (Exchangeable Image File) format. To read this information, you need software that enables you to extract the EXIF data. Most digital camera vendors provide image browser software that lets you read EXIF data while browsing thumbnail images. Also, you can read EXIF data from most image-management applications such as Cerious Software's ThumbsPlus (www.cerious.com) and ACD Systems's ACDSee (www.acdsystems.com). Adobe Photoshop Elements 2.0 and Photoshop 7 offer a file-browsing feature that you can use to view EXIF data. Additionally, some third-party vendors create free, specialized applications for reading and printing EXIF data, such as Thumber (www.tawbaware.com) and Exifer (www.exifer.friedemann.info).

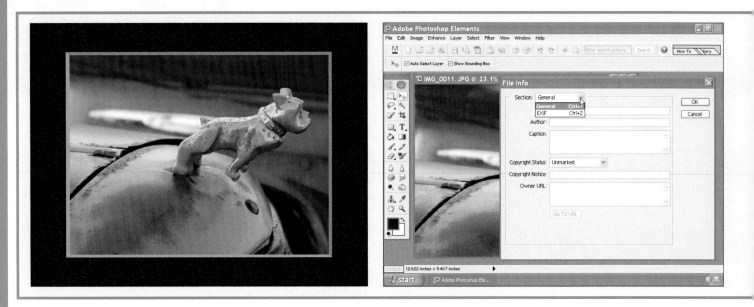

O Digital photo stored in a digital photo file formatted to the EXIF standard.

O To view the EXIF data of a file opened in Photoshop Elements 2.0, choose File ⇨ File Info and then click in the Section box to select EXIF (Ctrl+2).

Apply It! ☀

EXIF data can be useful for learning how to take better photos. After taking a few photos with different f-stops to control depth-of-field, or when shooting multiple shots with different exposures using exposure compensation, look at the image and the EXIF data to learn which settings were best.

Caution! ☀

Be careful when trying different EXIF-extraction tools and when using any features that rotate thumbnails or images contained inside the digital photo file. Some EXIF tools may make changes to your image files that make it impossible to read the EXIF data or even the image with other applications. Test new applications with duplicates of your original digital photo files.

DIFFICULTY LEVEL

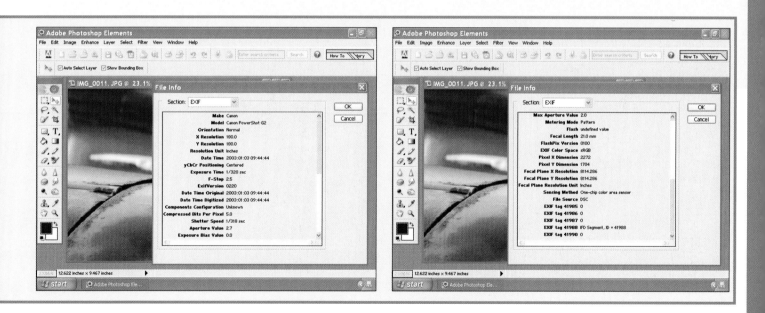

○ EXIF data shows this photo was taken with a Canon PowerShot G2 set to 1/320 @ f/2.5 with no exposure compensation.

○ EXIF data shows this photo was shot with a focal length of 21mm with the Pattern metering mode and sRGB color space.

Get good photos with
PATIENCE, PRACTICE, AND EFFORT

Photography is art. As is true with all art, the creation of good art takes patience, practice, and effort. Some amateur photographers buy expensive digital cameras and expect to immediately get wonderful photographs. After taking a few hundred photographs with minor success, they get discouraged and stop shooting. To prevent this from happening to you, use a good work ethic and patience to shoot lots of photographs, and you will see your efforts pay off.

Although a photographic vision of what you want to shoot and the ability to use your camera to capture that vision is essential to getting great shots, time spent shooting and patience to wait for the best shooting conditions significantly affect your photographic success.

Remember that when you shoot digitally, an important part of digital photography is editing with a digital photo editor like Adobe Photoshop Elements 2.0. After you shoot, open your photos in an image editor and work as hard to learn how to edit your photos as you do to take them.

O Take a hike to get you and your camera to new and exciting places to shoot.

O Great photos often require extraordinary effort like getting into a pond with hip waders to get close-up shots of a water lily.

Did You Know? ☀

Many professional photographers that shoot with a film camera shoot between 20 and 30 rolls of 36-exposure film per day, which equals about 700 to 1,000 photos per day. With digital cameras, the cost to shoot each photo is less, and you have the advantage of instantly viewing the photo you took.

Did You Know? ☀

One of the best ways to learn more about photography is to shoot often and shoot lots of pictures of the same subject or scene using different camera settings and compositions. Then, study the results by viewing them along with the EXIF data on your computer screen. If you did not get it right, try again until you get the shot you want.

DIFFICULTY LEVEL

O This photographer is patiently sitting while waiting for the perfect sunset at a well-chosen location.

O Studying images and EXIF data on a computer will help this photographer improve his picture-taking skills.

CHAPTER 3

Control Exposure

Many factors contribute to making a good photograph, but one of the most important factors is exposure. Although your camera's light meter can help you choose the right combination of shutter speed and aperture, and in some cases even the ISO speed, it can still misread the amount of light and give you a photo unlike what you have in mind. To improve your chances of getting the exposure you want, most digital cameras offer a wide range of features that can help considerably. Understanding features such as different exposure metering modes, histograms, exposure compensation, and manual mode can help you get the exposure you want.

Even the challenge of capturing the full range of brightness, from the darkest darks to the brightest highlights, is easier if you understand what you can do later with an image editor on your computer and you plan for combining two or more images. When it comes to getting the right exposure, the digital camera wins hands down over the film camera. Not only do you have all the incredibly useful features to help you get the right exposure, but you can instantly see the image on an LCD or view the histogram. If you are not happy with the picture you took, you can shoot until you get what you want — and it does not cost a thing!

TOP 100

Understanding
EXPOSURE
to get the photos you want

Exposure is the correct combination of shutter speed, aperture, and ISO speed needed to get the photograph you want. Exposure can be determined solely by the camera, by the photographer and the camera together, or solely by the photographer. Whenever the camera helps choose exposure settings, the camera's built-in light meter takes a reading of the reflected light in the scene and then sets appropriate camera settings.

When taking photos, remember that there is no such thing as a *perfect* exposure; only one that is how you want it to be. Overexposed photographs are overly light and detail is lost in the highlights. Underexposed photos are overly dark and detail is lost in the shadows.

Because digital camera exposure metering systems measure light as if it were reflected from a neutral-gray surface, they may misread the light when a scene is too dark or too light. Classic examples include a black cat sitting in front of a large pile of black coal, or a white cat sitting on snow.

UNDEREXPOSED

O Underexposing this photograph lead to a loss of detail in the shadow area.

PROPERLY EXPOSED

O This well-exposed photograph reveals details in the clouds in the highlight area and in the trees in the shadow area.

OVEREXPOSED

O Overexposing, or "washing out," this photograph causes loss of detail in the cloud area.

Did You Know? ☀

One of the significant advantages of using the RAW format (see task #4), if it is available on your digital camera, is that RAW conversion tools enable you to vary the exposure by +/– two f-stops. If you plan on using this feature, make sure that you do not overexpose the image and "blow out" the highlights (see task #24), because you will not be able to retrieve picture information in that area with a RAW conversion tool. See task 4 for more information on the RAW format.

Photo Tip! ☀

If you are shooting in a format other than RAW, or you are shooting a scene that may not meter correctly, consider using the *auto-bracketing* feature if it is available on your camera. Auto-bracketing enables you to shoot three sequential shots; the camera will automatically shoot at a user-selected f-stop and a plus and minus stop increment around the metered setting.

DIFFICULTY LEVEL

INCORRECT METERING

O This photo was not metered correctly and, as a result, reveals little visible detail in the black cat.

O This photo of two white cats shown against a black background was metered incorrectly, and the white cats appear gray.

O Photographers often incorrectly meter scenes with lots of white sand or snow, as is the case with this under-exposed photo of a snow-covered dairy farm.

Discover different
EXPOSURE MODES

Most digital cameras offer a variety of exposure modes including program or auto mode, shutter-priority, aperture-priority, manual, and bulb (time) modes. Choosing an exposure mode determines which exposure settings you can select and which, if any, exposure settings the camera will automatically select based upon the settings you have selected.

The camera automatically chooses both shutter speed and aperture settings when you select program or automatic mode. When using these modes on some cameras, you can *sometimes* modify these initial "camera-chosen" settings.

When you select shutter-priority mode, the camera automatically chooses the aperture setting to get a good exposure. Likewise, when you choose aperture-priority mode, choose the aperture setting you want, and the camera will select the appropriate shutter speed. Remember when you use these modes to choose the shutter speed setting when using shutter-priority mode, and choose the aperture setting when you use aperture-priority mode; otherwise, you will simply be using the last setting that was used. In those situations where you want complete control over both shutter speed and aperture, choose manual mode.

○ You usually select an exposure mode by turning a dial like this one found on the Canon PowerShot G2.

○ For snapshot photos and general use, select program or automatic exposure mode.

Did You Know? ☼

Automatic shooting modes such as landscape, macro, and portrait modes often result in a good photograph. Automatic shooting modes may not produce the best possible photos, however, if you understand and can correctly use the shutter-priority or aperture-priority mode settings.

Caution! ☼

Some shooting modes such as program or automatic mode allow the camera to automatically change the ISO setting if a change is needed. When you use a faster ISO speed, there will be more digital noise in the image. If you do not want to have excess digital noise, make sure you know when to avoid using a mode that allows automatic ISO speed changes.

PRIORITY MODES

O Choose aperture-priority mode when you want to control depth-of-field; in this mode, the camera automatically sets its shutter speed.

O Choose shutter-priority mode when you want to control shutter speed; the camera then automatically sets the aperture.

O Use manual mode when you want complete control over both shutter speed and aperture.

Choose an appropriate exposure
METERING MODE

Today's digital cameras have a built-in exposure meter that measures the amount of reflected light from a scene to determine the appropriate settings to get a medium-toned exposure. Although built-in exposure meters are getting increasingly sophisticated, they can take readings that do not provide the exposure that you want. In many cases, these "bad" readings are caused by reading either too much or too little light from the scene. To give the photographer more control over what light is metered, most digital cameras offer more than one exposure meter mode.

Some of the more common exposure meter modes are *averaging* or *multi-segment, center-weighted,* or *spot*. The most useful is the averaging or multisegment mode, which takes a reading from the entire area shown in your composition. The center-weighted mode places more emphasis on the center of the image, and spot metering reads only a tiny part of the image. Picking the most appropriate exposure-metering mode increases the chance you will get the exposure you want.

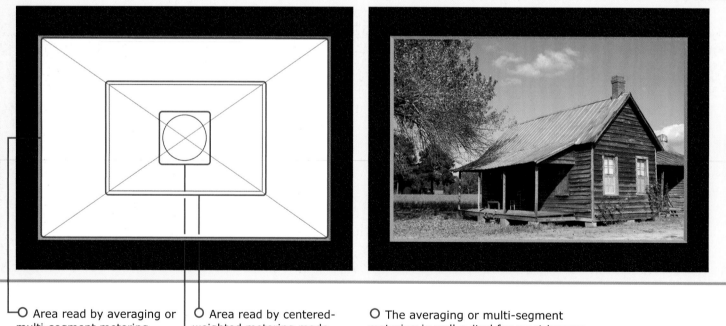

O Area read by averaging or multi-segment metering mode.

O Area read by centered-weighted metering mode.

O Area read by spot metering mode.

O The averaging or multi-segment metering is well suited for most images like this medium-toned photo of a farm house.

Did You Know? ☀

Many digital cameras have selectable auto-focus points that allow you to focus on off-center subjects. If your camera has this feature, check to see if one of your metering modes is linked to the selectable auto-focus points. This feature makes it easy to focus on an off-center subject like the tree photo that was shot from inside a cave, shown below, and to meter the light from that same point.

Photo Tip! ☀

When your chosen exposure-metering mode does not result in the exposure you want, you have two choices. You can adjust the exposure either by using exposure compensation (see task #23) or by using manual mode, where you choose both the aperture and shutter speed settings without any assistance from the built-in meter.

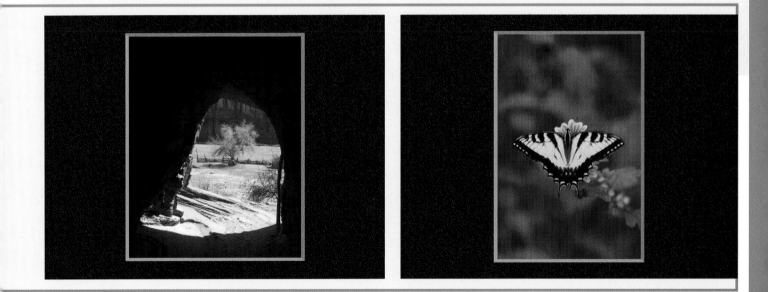

O The center-weighted metering mode is useful for reading light on images like this one where the background illumination is not to be metered.

O This butterfly was metered correctly using the spot metering mode to avoid taking into account the abundance of dark background.

Using the
HISTOGRAM
to get the exposure you want

One of the most useful features found on some, but not all, digital cameras is the histogram. The *histogram* is a graphical chart that shows the brightness levels of an image ranging from pure black on the left to pure white on the right in 256 steps. The vertical scale shows how many pixels are found in the image at each brightness level.

Using the histogram, you can easily read the exposure of a photo. The more pixels there are to the right, the brighter the image is. Conversely, the more pixels there are to the left, the darker the

image will be. The histogram also gives you a clear indication when you have *blown-out* highlights (see task #24), which in most cases you want to avoid.

Although it is tempting to shoot to get a perfect histogram — that is, one nicely centered and dispersed across the full brightness range — such a histogram does not mean it is a good exposure. The example photos and histogram shown below illustrate the importance of getting the right histogram for the subject and your intended exposure.

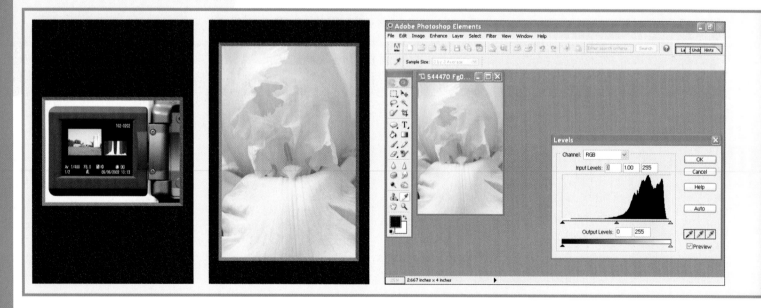

O The Canon PowerShot G2 digital camera shows a histogram along with a small thumbnail image and important camera settings on an LCD screen.

O This pure white iris was correctly exposed using a built-in metering mode, a histogram, and exposure compensation.

O This histogram of the white iris indicates a correctly exposed image, as the image is skewed to the bright side of the tonal range to keep the white iris white.

#22

Caution! ☀

Many digital cameras enable you to change the brightness of the LCD screen used to view images that you are about to take or have taken. Changing the brightness level or viewing the screen in bright light can cause you to misread exposure. If your camera offers a histogram, you can use its graphical chart to give you an accurate view of exposure, regardless of the LCD screen brightness setting or bright light.

Did You Know? ☀

Digital photo editors like Adobe Photoshop Elements have a feature that is similar to the histogram on some digital cameras for reading overall brightness of an image. The Levels command provides a histogram along with the ability to modify tonal range and overall image contrast.

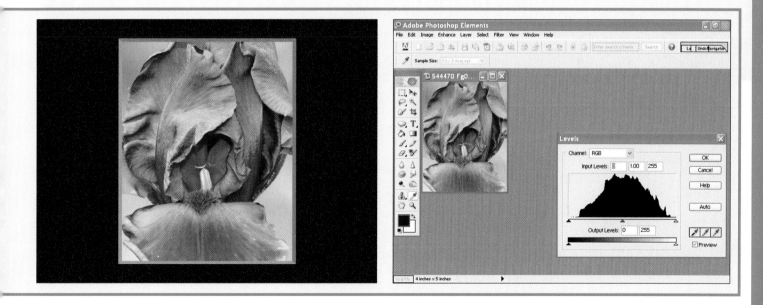

O This nearly solid black "Black Beauty" iris was incorrectly exposed as a medium tone, which makes it appear purple rather than black.

O This Adobe Photoshop Elements Levels histogram shows how there are no black or near-black tones in the Black Beauty iris photo.

Improve exposure with
EXPOSURE COMPENSATION

In some cases, the built-in light meter in your camera results in a bad exposure even if you chose a reasonable exposure mode (see task #20) and you picked the most appropriate metering mode (see task #21). To get a good exposure in these cases, use exposure compensation if your camera offers that feature.

Exposure compensation allows you to modify the exposure up or down from the metered reading by a specified amount. By doing this, you can continue shooting using the compensated setting and get good exposures. For example, if the meter reading indicates the need for a shutter speed of $\frac{1}{60}$ of a second at f/5.6, a +1 exposure compensation would modify the aperture setting to f/4.0 if shutter-priority mode was selected, or to $\frac{1}{30}$ of a second if aperture-priority mode was selected.

Using exposure compensation can be particularly useful when shooting in bright areas like beaches or when snow fills most of the scene, or when shooting in a backlit situation where light comes from behind the subject leaving the subject in the shadow and the background bright.

METERED SETTINGS

O This photo was shot using the metered settings and it metered too much light, causing an underexposed photo.

+1

O This photo was shot with a +1 exposure compensation setting, which resulted in a reasonably good exposure.

23

DIFFICULTY LEVEL

Did You Know? ※

Using an exposure-compensation feature is the easy way to modify the built-in metering system to get the exposures you want. If, for example, you are shooting a scene that is covered in snow, you can dial in the exposure compensation setting to adjust the built-in meter so that you get perfect photographs each time you press the shutter release.

Photo Tip! ※

There may be times when you want to shoot with more than a +2 or -2 exposure compensation. In those cases, you should choose the manual shooting mode. If the desired exposure compensation is outside the range of your camera, you may need to change the ISO setting.

+1⅓

O This photo was shot with a +1⅓ exposure compensation setting, resulting in a good exposure.

+2

O This photo was shot with a +2 exposure compensation setting, which results in the best exposure.

Avoid blown-out
HIGHLIGHTS

If any photography rule should not be broken (well, most of the time), it is that you should avoid *blown-out* highlights, unless you want them for creative reasons. A blown-out highlight occurs when you use exposure settings that make part of the image pure white where there should be details.

The problem with pure white has to do with the mathematics of a digital photograph. Although you can usually bring back detail that is in nearly black or shadow areas, you cannot bring out detail that is

pure white using a digital image editor such as Adobe Photoshop Elements.

If your camera LCD has a histogram, it likely also has a *highlight alert*, which is a feature that shows blinking bright white pixels on a thumbnail image. These blinking white pixels mean you need to decrease the exposure until there are no more blown-out highlights. If a histogram shows a number of pixels at the extreme right, then this is also an indication that you need to reduce your exposure.

O This horse photo has been overexposed, as the pure white area on the face has no detail that can be brought back into the photo with an image editor.

O This histogram shows how much of the detail in the horse's face has been pushed into the detail-less highlight area.

Did You Know? ☀

When shooting with a digital camera, you should usually use exposure settings to properly expose for the highlight area of a scene. Using an image editor such as Adobe Photoshop Elements, you can often bring details back into an underexposed area; you cannot, however, bring detail back from an overexposed highlight area where all the details are blown out because there are few or no details in the near-white or pure white areas.

Did You Know? ☀

One place that pure white is acceptable is where there are spectral highlights. A spectral highlight is a bright spot from a shiny, highly reflective surface. Generally, spectral highlights should be small and very focused.

DIFFICULTY LEVEL

O The pure white spectral highlights or reflections on this well-exposed photo of the shiny steel headlight are correct.

O The smooth white marble on the top of the head and on the arm of this statue should be pure white, as there is no detail to show.

Understanding
DYNAMIC RANGE

Photography and print professionals refer to the range between the darkest parts of an image and the lightest parts of an image as the *dynamic* or *tonal range.* A composition that has very bright parts such as a sky and very dark parts where there are deep shadows is said to have a wide dynamic range. Unfortunately, no film or digital cameras can capture such a wide dynamic range.

You may think that a photo that has too wide a dynamic range that was exposed for the highlights

would not show any black at all, even if it were in the scene. On the contrary, the shadow area tones are compressed into fewer tonal ranges, making them show little or no detail. Conversely, if you expose for the shadow area, the highlight area is compressed with little highlight detail.

O This photo reveals detail in the white sign but not in the bird's dark feathers, because the dynamic range is too wide.

O This histogram represents the tonal range of the photo on the left.

#25

DIFFICULTY LEVEL

Did You Know? ※

Many film photographers use a graduated neutral density filter to enable them to capture a wide dynamic range. Although this filter, which gradually changes from dark to light in a vertical direction, helps to capture a wide dynamic range, it does so in a less realistic manner than you can do when combining two images with a digital photo editor (see task #26).

Photo Tip! ※

You can expose a scene with a wide dynamic range to get excellent silhouettes (see task #39). You can also shoot to expose the shadows in a landscape photo to make a bright white sky become a blown-out highlight, which makes it very easy to replace with a new and better sky by using a selection tool in an image editor and selecting the pure white area.

O This is a classic example of the difficulty of getting details in a bright sky and in the darker foreground.

O The bright white sky limits how much detail in the boats is shown.

Combine two photos to get
FULL DYNAMIC RANGE

One of the great things about digital photography is that there is virtually no limit to what you can do with one or more photos when you are skilled with an image editor. When you are shooting a challenging composition that has a wide dynamic range, you can make an image that shows the full dynamic range in one of two ways.

First, you can shoot two separate photos — one exposed for the shadows and one for the highlights — and then combine them with an image editor. To

get the photos to match up exactly, you need to use a tripod and you need to shoot without any moving objects in the scene.

Alternatively, you can take one photo using RAW format and use a RAW converter such as the Adobe Photoshop Camera RAW plug-in to convert the photo twice. First, convert it using an exposure setting to expose for the highlights and then convert it to expose for the shadows. Finally, use an image editor to combine the photos.

○ This photo was exposed to capture detail in the shadow area or the foreground.

○ This photo was exposed to capture detail in the highlight area so that there is good detail in the clouds in the sky.

○ Combining the first two photos using an image editor allows the full dynamic range to be shown.

#26

DIFFICULTY LEVEL

Did You Know? ⁂

You may have more visible dynamic range in your digital photos than you can see. A good-quality computer monitor that has been carefully calibrated using Adobe Gamma or some other utility to show a wide dynamic range is essential to seeing and properly editing digital photos.

Photo Tip! ⁂

In many cases, you will not be able to take two photographs set to different exposures so that they can be combined. Examples include scenes with moving subjects such as fast-moving clouds or wildlife. In those cases, shoot using the RAW format and change the exposure using a converter.

○ This photo was recorded in the RAW format and later converted to expose detail in the shadow area or the foreground.

○ This photo was recorded in the RAW format and later converted to show good detail in the clouds in the sky.

○ The two images on the left were combined using an image editor to show the full dynamic range.

CHAPTER 4

Control Focus and Depth of Field

Incorrect focus control, limited depth of field, subject movement, or camera movement can all cause a blurry photo. Sometimes you may intend to have blur in a photo while other times it is an unwanted characteristic of a "not quite right" photo. To get photos you want, you need to be able to control focus and depth of field.

These two important photography variables impact each and every photo you take. Although you need to understand how to control focus and depth of field, and to understand the various tradeoffs you are faced with when making one decision over another, it is also equally important to be able to visualize the effect you will get. For example, you need to be

able to have a good idea of how much depth of field you will have when shooting with a 100mm lens 4 feet away from the subject using an aperture setting of f/4 instead of f/8. The more you shoot and study your shots with the EXIF data, the better you will get at choosing the settings and setting up to get the photographs you want. See task #17 to learn more about EXIF data.

Focus and depth of field are two variables that enable the digital photographer to shoot more creatively. To develop the "mental view," shoot a few series of photos of various combinations of these variables and then study them carefully.

TOP 100

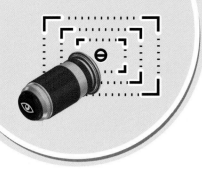

ACHIEVE SHARP FOCUS
using a tripod

If you shoot with low light levels, slow shutter speeds, or you want to maximize depth of field by shooting with a small aperture, you will need to use a tripod to take sharply focused photos. The longer the focal length of lens you use, the more important it is to use a tripod, because even the slightest movement can blur a photo. Besides enabling you to consistently take sharply focused photos, a tripod also makes it easy for you to shoot a more precisely and carefully composed photo.

Carrying and using a tripod can initially be bothersome. However, if you select a good tripod and head, and you get used to using it and taking sharply focused photos, it will be hard for you to take photos without one. If you plan on shooting panoramas (see task #52), consider getting a tripod head that has an independent panning feature like the Manfrotto 488RC2 (www.manfrotto.com) shown here. Photographers who regularly use a tripod get better photographs. If you are not using one, get one and use it.

Photo courtesy Bogen Photo, Ramsey, NJ

Photo courtesy Bogen Photo, Ramsey, NJ

Photo courtesy Bogen Photo, Ramsey, NJ

○ A solid tripod like the Manfrotto 3221WN Tripod is helpful for getting sharply focused and well-composed photos.

○ The Manfrotto #352 ball head is a lightweight, easy to use ball head.

○ The Manfrotto 488RC2 ball head has a separate lever and a graduated scale for panning. A quick-release lets you quickly and easily mount a camera on a tripod.

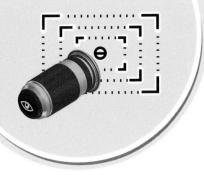

Control focus with FOCUS AREA SELECTION

DIFFICULTY LEVEL

The shallower the depth of field, the more important it is to precisely select the part of the composition that you want clearly focused. If you are shooting a composition that has an off-center element that should be in focus, check your camera manual to learn about the features it has for selecting the focus area.

There are three common types of features for selecting focus area. Some cameras have a *fixed focus point*, usually in the center. With a *center focus point*, you aim

that point on the subject where you want critical focus, press the shutter button halfway to use automatic focus, recompose the picture, and then press the shutter button the rest of the way to take a picture. Some cameras enable you to select anywhere from 3 to as many as 50 focus points. After selecting the focus point, you simply compose and take the picture. Many cameras also have *automatic focus point selection*, which, surprisingly, often picks the best focus point for the subject.

O An off-center focus point keeps the lady examining necklaces in focus.

O Aiming the center focus point on the shack and locking focus keeps this red crab shack in focus.

O The photo was then recomposed and the shutter release button pressed all the way down to capture the image.

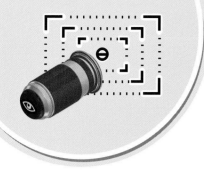

SHOW ACTION
using a slow shutter speed

DIFFICULTY LEVEL

Usually, the objective is to use a shutter speed that is fast enough to stop any action in a photograph. However, you can use a slow enough shutter speed that your subject is partly blurred to show movement. To avoid getting a blurred background in addition to a blurrred subject due to the slow shutter speed, use a tripod to limit the blur to the moving subject.

Choosing the right shutter speed is critical. Choosing one that is too slow yields too much blur. Choosing one that is too fast eliminates any sense of movement. With a little experimentation, you can learn which shutter speeds you need to get the results you want.

If there is too much bright light, your camera may not have a small enough aperture setting to show motion. In such cases, you can either shoot when there is less bright light, or you can use a neutral density filter to block some of the light entering the camera, which enables you to choose a slower shutter speed. To learn more about photographing with a neutral density filter, turn to task #50.

O These magnificent horses look even more magnificent in this photo taken at 1/30th of a second to reveal the speed of their gallop.

O The action shown in this photo of a boy jumping shows how much fun he was having and how much effort he expended.

O In bright sunlight, a very slow shutter speed can even slow the propeller of an airplane taxiing on a runway.

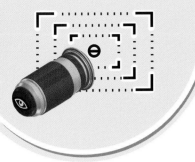

ADD DRAMA
by panning with the subject

#30

Another technique for showing action is to pan the camera with a horizontally moving subject. The result can be a dramatic photo showing the subject clearly focused against a nicely blurred background that is blurred horizontally.

The challenging parts of this technique are to choose the right shutter speed, pick the right background, and to pan with the subject so that the moving subject is not blurred due to a panning speed that does not match the speed of the moving subject.

Getting the effect you want when panning with a camera requires considerable experimentation

and some skill, so you will need to practice. You must consider many variables, including the speed of the moving subject, the distances between the subject and the photographer, the distance between the subject and the background, focal length, shutter speed, and the capabilities of your camera. Additionally, you need to be able to skillfully pan with the subject. Using a tripod head that has independent panning motion or a fluid head video camera tripod head can be useful for getting well-panned photographs.

○ A shutter speed of 1/30 enabled this horse to be photographed so that both the background and horse are blurred to show motion.

○ A slow shutter speed of 1/125 was selected to freeze the flying pelican against the wonderfully colored and blurred background of a seaside harbor.

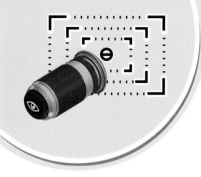

CONTROL FOCUS CREATIVELY
with manual focus

A flawlessly in-focus photo may not always be what you want. Imaginative photographers experiment with all the photography variables to get new and exciting photographs. Focus is one of those variables that you can change to dramatically alter a picture. A soft, out-of-focus photo can result in a mood that cannot be shown in a well-focused photo of the same subject. Likewise, you can carefully control focus to place emphasis on the subject or an important part of a composition.

When your intent is to either take a picture that is out-of-focus, or you want to have precise control over focus and where to position the depth of field, use manual focus to get exactly what you want. Freeing yourself from one more automatic feature helps you to thoroughly think through another important aspect of your photography — focus. Try setting your camera to manual focus and use it to be more creative.

O Manual focus made it easy to control precisely where the shallow depth of field was positioned on these soft-focused tulips.

O Here, manual focus gives the photographer precise control over which part of the bee is in focus.

Did You Know?

Some of the world's greatest photographs have been taken with cameras that were manually focused because automatically focusing cameras were not available. In those early days, professional photographers worked hard to refine their picture-taking skills, and their success remains as proof that expensive, feature-rich cameras are not essential to take great photographs.

Photo Tip!

Precise manual focus is difficult to get with many compact digital cameras. If you are having problems focusing in manual mode, consider getting a macro positioning rail like the Manfrotto (www.manfrotto.com) 3419 Micro Positioning Plate. This tripod head accessory allows you to move your camera forwards or backwards using a dial to get perfect focus distance without having to move your tripod.

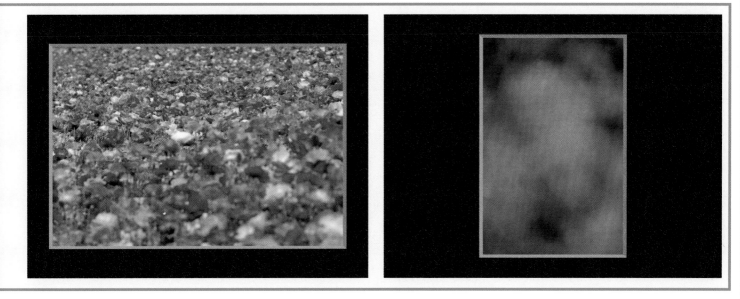

○ Getting the intended area of the tulips in focus in this photo was easy with the camera set to manual focus.

○ This intentionally out-of-focus photo of purple flowers was taken to combine with another photograph with an image editor.

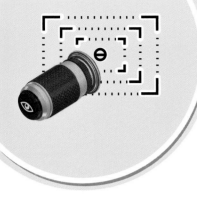

DEPTH OF FIELD

Depth of field is the area in a photograph that is in focus. It is determined by three primary factors: the aperture setting, the distance to the subject, and the focal length. The smaller the aperture opening, the more depth of field you will have. For example, an f-stop of f/4.0 will be larger than an f-stop of f/8.0, and it will consequently have less depth of field. As the distance from the camera to the subject increases, so will the depth of field. Lenses with longer focal lengths have a shallower depth of field

than a lens with a short focal length. For example, a 100mm lens has considerably less depth of field than a 28mm lens.

Clearly understanding and being able to control depth of field is a significant part of photography. Besides using depth of field to isolate a subject from its background or to ensure that everything in the picture is sharply focused to show as much detail as is possible, there are many other creative uses as well.

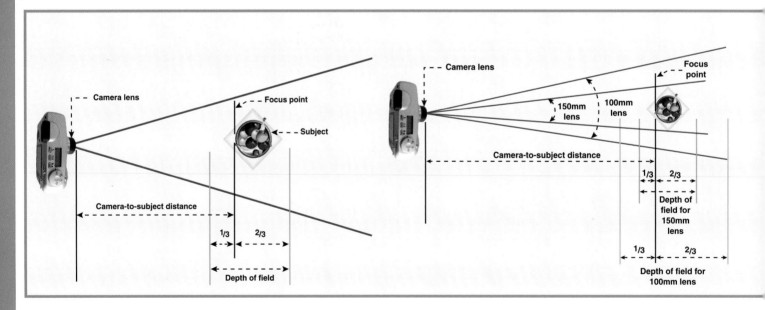

O One-third of the depth of field is in front of the focus point and two-thirds is behind the focus point.

O Shorter focal length lenses (35mm) have more depth of field than long focal length lenses (100mm) when the camera-to-subject distance is equal.

Did You Know?

The larger the aperture, the "faster" the lens is considered because it lets in more light than a slower lens or one with a smaller aperture. Most fast lenses cost more than slow lenses.

Photo Tip!

When you want maximum depth of field and are shooting in low light, or you are shooting close-up or macro shots, the movement of the camera caused by pressing the shutter release button can cause unwanted image blur. To avoid camera movement caused by pressing the shutter button, set the timer-release so that the camera takes a photo without you pressing the shutter release button.

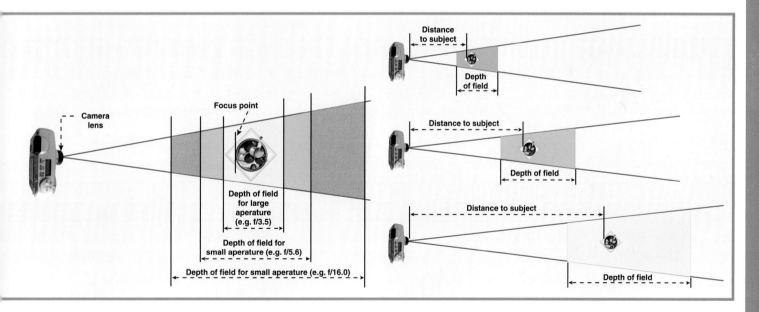

○ Aperture size is one determinant of depth of field. Small apertures result in greater depth of fields. A wide-angle lens has more depth of field than a telephoto lens.

○ Camera-to-subject distance is one of three factors that affect depth of field. The farther away a subject is from the camera, the greater the depth of field will be.

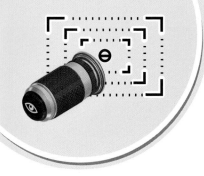

CREATE COOL EFFECTS
with depth of field

Depth of field is determined by three factors: how close you are to the subject, what focal length lens you are using, and what aperture setting you are using. The farther away you are from the point where you set focus, the deeper the depth of field will be. The longer the focal length you use, the shallower the depth of field will be. The smaller the aperture you use, the more depth of field you will have. You need to understand the relationships between all three of these factors to effectively control depth of field.

Photography is all about controlling a wide range of variables and understanding the trade-offs when choosing settings. When you use a longer focal length lens to get a shallower depth of field, you will be able to show less of the subject due to a smaller angle of view. Using a smaller aperture to get more depth of field will require a longer exposure. Shooting farther away from the subject makes it harder to get a tightly cropped subject.

○ Using a lens with a long focal length, and by selecting a large aperture to get a shallow depth of field isolates these three flowers from the background.

○ A wide-angle lens with a small aperture was used to keep the entire archway photo in focus. A tripod was also used to minimize camera movement that would have blurred the shot with the required slow shutter speed.

Did You Know?

Because of the small size of the image sensor used in many compact digital cameras, it is very hard to control depth of field, because any of the available aperture settings produce rather deep depth of fields. If you mostly want to shoot photos with little blur due to shallow depth of fields, such a camera is wonderful. If instead, you want to be able to shoot subjects with blurred backgrounds, you may need to buy a digital SLR that allows you to shoot with a small depth of field.

Photo Tip!

When you are taking a portrait, try using a long focal length to get a small depth of field to focus attention on your subject and get a soft blurred background.

O A wide-angle lens made with deep depth of field made it easy to keep all of the pumpkins and the pumpkin stand in focus in this photo.

O Depth of field is very shallow when shooting close up to a subject like this dragonfly with a long telephoto lens, and when using a mid-range aperture to minimize subject movement caused by wind.

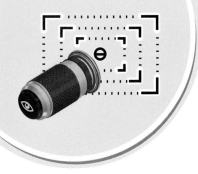

Understanding
FOCAL LENGTH

Technically, focal length is the distance in millimeters between the optical center of the lens and the image sensor in a digital camera when the lens is focused on infinity. However, focal length by itself *does not* describe the angle of view as is commonly thought. The angle of view is highly dependent on *both* the focal length and the size of the image sensor on which the lens focuses its image.

To make it easy to compare angles of view, the camera industry is fast accepting the term "35mm

equivalent focal length." Long focal-length lenses such as a 200mm "35mm equivalent focal length" have a narrower angle of view than lenses with a shorter focal length like 50mm. To capture a wider angle of view, you need a wide-angle lens. To get really wide-angle photographs, you can shoot multiple photos and digitally stitch them together; see task #52 to shoot multiple photos to make a panorama.

"35mm Equivalent Focal Length" is equal to the focal length of the lens X the camera's "focal length multiplier"

Photo courtesy of Nikon, Inc.

○ You can usually find the focal length multiplier for your camera in your camera's documentation.

○ The Nikon Coolpix 5700 has a zoom lens with focal length noted as 8.9mm to 71.2mm. The focal length multiplier is 3.93. The 35mm equivalent focal length is 35 (3.93 x 8.9) to 280mm (3.93 x 71.2).

DIFFICULTY LEVEL

Did You Know?

Many zoom cameras have an X-rating, like 2X or 4X, which is not directly related to the focal length. It just means that the maximum focal length is "X-times" longer than the minimum focal length. For example, the Nikon Coolpix 5700 has a 4X zoom lens, which simply means that the longest focal length is "4 times" longer than the shortest focal length.

Photo Tip!

Some digital cameras have a digital zoom feature that gives you even longer focal length than you get with the optical zoom. *Optical zoom* is done solely through the optics of the lens. *Digital zoom* is actually the center of the composition enlarged digitally and it is extremely inferior to optical zoom.

NIKON COOLPIX 5700 ZOOM LENS

O This photo demonstrates the shortest focal length, 35mm.

O An intermediate zoom.

O The Coolpix 5700 zoomed in even more.

O This photo shows the longest focal length of 280mm.

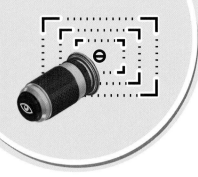

CONTROL PERSPECTIVE

with focal length

When you stand in the middle of railroad tracks that vanish into the horizon, you are experiencing *perspective.* When you experience perspective, straight lines converge over distance. When shooting photos with a camera, you can use focal length to control how rapidly parallel lines converge or if they converge at all. The shorter the focal length, the more rapidly parallel lines converge.

To shoot a full-frame picture of a large building with a wide-angle lens, you have to be fairly close, and the building's lines will tend to converge over a short distance. If you shoot farther back from the building with a telephoto lens, you can still fill the frame, but you can do so without allowing perspective to make the building look distorted due to rapidly converging lines that are really parallel lines.

Unfortunately, many of the zoom lenses on compact digital cameras suffer from "barrel" or "pin-cushion" distortion. These distortions are in addition to the convergence of parallel lines, and they result in lines that either curve in or curve out instead of remaining straight.

O The façade of this office building shows severe convergence of parallel horizontal lines because it was taken up close and with a wide-angle lens.

O The white grid laid over this building shows the virtual curving of lines that should be straight. This distortion is caused by a wide-angle lens.

#35

DIFFICULTY LEVEL

Did You Know?

Several software applications are available to correct various types of image distortion such as barrel and pin-cushion distortion, which are caused by wide-angle lenses. One product is LensDoc from Andromeda Software Inc. (www.andromeda.com). It offers specific corrections for many specific camera models and there is a version for PC and Mac.

Did You Know?

You can use an image editor like Adobe Photoshop Elements to correct the convergence of lines in a photo taken with a wide-angle lens. Choose Image, Transform, and then Perspective to make lines that should be parallel — parallel.

O This photo was taken with a wide-angle lens to include the house and a wide expanse of the sky and the tree.

O More perspective distortion is noticed in this house than the one on the left, because the photo was taken close to the house.

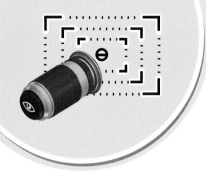

CONTROL
BACKGROUND
with focal length and aperture

Controlling the background in a photo is often a key factor in getting a good composition. You can easily control the background with a long focal length lens, which has a shallow depth of field and a narrow angle of view. The shallow depth of field helps to create a soft-focused background. The narrow view makes it easier to change the background by moving the camera location to the left or right, or even up or down a few inches, with minimal effect on the composition of the subject.

Several factors determine how much you can control the background. The distance from the camera to the subject, and the distance between the subject and the background are two important factors along with the focal length. The closer the camera is to the subject, the narrower the depth of field will be, which helps to blur the background. Likewise, the farther the background is from the subject, the more you can blur the background. A tripod is a good aid to precise composition and successful control of the background when shooting with a long focal length lens.

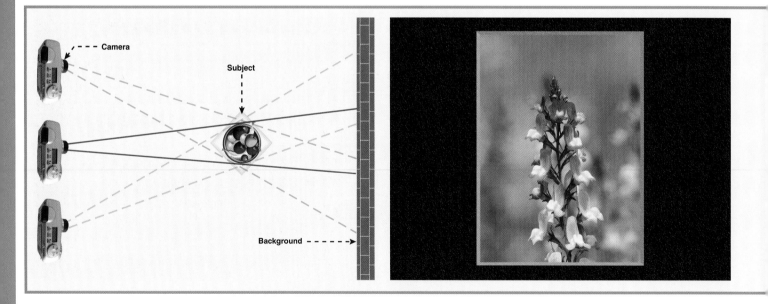

○ The longer the focal length of a lens, the more a slight move to the right or left may change the background.

○ The flowers in the foreground are lost in the background in this photo.

Photo Tip

Greatest depth of field is obtained by selecting the smallest aperture. When shooting with a small aperture, you need to use a slower shutter speed to get a proper exposure. This is the reason why you need to use a tripod when the objective is to shoot with maximum depth of field.

Did You Know?

Aperture settings are written as f/4.0 or f/8.0. But, in fact, the aperture size is really $\frac{1}{4.0}$ or $\frac{1}{4}$, and $\frac{1}{8.0}$ or $\frac{1}{8}$, which means that an f/4.0 aperture is actually larger than an f/8.0 aperture, because one-fourth is larger than one-eighth.

O The softly blurred background with contrasting colors helps to isolate and focus attention on the flowers in the foreground.

O The closer the background is to the subject, the more difficult it is to get a softly blurred background.

CHAPTER 5

Shoot in Good Light

Although your natural inclination may be to focus your attention on your subject and compose carefully to get the shots you want, you can greatly improve your photography if you put an equal amount of time into evaluating and controlling light. What often distinguishes really good photographs from all the rest is how light is used to capture the photograph. Depending upon the kinds of subjects you shoot, you may need to work exclusively with natural light, or you may be able to use a combination of natural and artificial light.

After you have decided what you want to shoot, and you have a vision for the kind of shots you want, carefully consider the characteristics of the available light if you are shooting with natural light. Do you have backlighting, front lighting, or does the light come in from the side? Does the light come in from a low angle or is the sun high in the sky? Is the light soft and diffused, or is it bright and intense? Does the light have a warm golden glow or maybe another color cast?

When you do not have good light, consider ways in which you may improve it, or find another time to try again. Can you use one or more flashes? Are you shooting close-ups where a macro ring light might be the most effective kind of supplemental light? Would one or more hand-held light reflectors be useful? The more you take advantage of good light, the better your photos will be.

TOP 100

PICK GOOD LIGHT
for better photos

Digital photography is all about capturing light on an image sensor; the better the light, the more potential you have for getting great photographs. The quality of light can vary greatly from when the sun comes up in the morning to when it sets in the evening. Sometimes it varies on a second-by-second basis, such as when there are fast-moving clouds. The best way to learn what light is good light for the subjects you enjoy shooting is to shoot frequently and carefully study your photographs. Learn to judge light on direction, intensity, and color, and use that information to decide when and where to shoot.

One caveat for the serious outdoor photographer intent on shooting with only the best light: The best light conditions are rare. You must have time and patience to wait for those perfect moments to capture a perfect shot. If you have limited time or patience, you simply have to have good luck to be at the right place at the right time.

○ Heavy cloud cover and late evening sunlight help silhouette the tractor in this photo.

○ Fog reduces the dynamic range of light, which results in soft smooth gradations like this photo of a swamp.

○ The low light of evening helps to give this swamp photo a golden glow against a rich blue sky with puffy white clouds.

#37

DIFFICULTY LEVEL

Did You Know? ※

Bad weather conditions can often make for better photographic opportunities than good weather with blue skies. Look for dramatic clouds, thunderstorms, lightning, or windstorms that fill the air with dust. Changing weather conditions are also a good time to shoot. Try to capture an opening in the sky filled with blue sky against an oncoming rainstorm.

Photo Tip! ※

Clouds can be very helpful to photographers because they can diffuse bright sun and reduce the overall light intensity and contrast. Clouds can make an otherwise clear sky into a more interesting sky. Use clouds to your advantage and have patience for them to move to where they will help you get better photographs.

○ Rich fall colors can sometimes be so strong that they can cast light when sunlight is not too bright.

○ The soft early morning light on this iris photo makes it easy to capture the bright and shadowy parts of this iris.

○ Even the golden glow of incandescent light against rich wood colors can create wonderful light in an interior like this one.

Shoot
HAZE OR FOG

DIFFICULTY LEVEL

Do not avoid taking photos just because haze or fog is present. Haze or fog can act as an excellent light diffuser that can help you get some wonderful photos. Besides helping to reduce the overall contrast of an image, haze and fog can create an atmosphere that may transform what would otherwise be an uninteresting scene into a wonderful photograph.

When properly exposing haze or fog, you can get wonderful silhouettes and smooth monotone gradations that can make a photograph both simple and powerful. It can also add some

mystery to the photo, as a viewer may not be able to see much detail in the photograph. Whenever you have a chance to shoot in haze or fog, take it. Make sure, however, that you understand how to use exposure compensation, because your camera's built-in light meter will likely give you an exposure that is not what you want. For a detailed explanation of exposure compensation, see task #23.

You can use a digital image editor like Adobe Photoshop Element to further refine your haze or fog photos into spectacular images.

O The haze seen from the Smokey Mountains makes photographs like this one rich in soft subtle gradations that diminish with distance.

O The fog at this swamp combined with the late evening sun to help create a wonderful monotone of silhouettes of trees in the water.

SILHOUETTE
your subject

Backlighting occurs when your subject has a bright light in back of it, often resulting in dark shadows on the subject. Shooting in this kind of lighting can be both challenging and rewarding. The often extreme contrast between the bright background and an unlit subject makes it possible to get a silhouette.

Getting a good exposure in a backlit situation can be challenging. Shoot a couple of photos with different settings and compare the results on your LCD screen. If your camera offers a histogram (see task #22), you can use it to see

if you have a dark or nearly black silhouetted subject, or if you have blown-out highlights (see task #24) in the bright areas of the composition.

After you have taken a silhouette, you can use an image editor like Adobe Photoshop Elements to further refine the image and turn it into an excellent print. You can use the Set Black Point eyedropper tool found in the Levels dialog box to make the silhouetted subject pure black by selecting the eyedropper and clicking on the area that is silhouetted.

DIFFICULTY LEVEL

O The fading sunlight behind the trees produced this silhouette.

O This silhouette of a flying pelican was made because of the extreme contrast between the dark pelican and the bright sky.

Learn when to shoot with a BUILT-IN FLASH

DIFFICULTY LEVEL

Cameras with a built-in flash are very useful when you take snapshots, or when you must take a photo and there is not enough light and you cannot add light in any other way. Otherwise, you should carefully consider ways to avoid using a built-in flash most of the time. A built-in flash lights your subject with unnatural light that comes straight from the camera. The resulting effect is that important shadows, which add dimension to your subject, are removed by the flash. The use of an external flash has the benefit of projecting light on a subject from an angle that helps maintain important subtle shadows.

If your camera has *flash exposure compensation,* which enables you to reduce the balance of flash relative to natural light, you can use *fill-flash* (see task #41) to lighten some of the darker shadows to reveal details while keeping some shadow to add dimension to the subject. You can also use a built-in flash to provide a *catch-light* (see task #42) to any subject with eyes and to stop motion.

O This photo taken without a flash shows good dimension and natural colors.

O The use of built-in flash for this photo has diminished the shadows resulting in a flat-looking image with less natural colors.

Reveal detail with a
FILL FLASH

#41

Fill flash is light from a built-in or external flash that is used to illuminate dark shadows to reveal detail, and to reduce overall image contrast in bright sun. When you are shooting compositions with strong shadows or backlighting, consider using fill flash.

When you shoot a backlit subject where the primary light source is behind your subject and in front of you, the result can be extremely high contrast. Fill flash can reduce image contrast while lighting your subject to reveal important details. Most backlit subjects are challenging to meter, so try a few different flash and exposure settings to get the photo you want.

If your camera has exposure compensation, you can use that feature to get the best balance between existing light and light from the flash. The closer you are to the subject, the more important it is to use exposure compensation to reduce the overall power of your flash so that you do not overwhelm your subject with bright artificial light.

○ Canon 550EX Speedlite mounted on a Canon PowerShot G2.

○ Bright sun creates extreme contrast on this iris with well-lit areas and dark detail-less shadow areas.

○ A fill flash reduces overall contrast and lights the shadowy areas to reveal detail in this iris.

Add a catch light to
SUBJECTS' EYES

Generally, whenever you are shooting a subject with eyes, you should try to keep the eyes in focus and capture a sparkle or *catch light* in them. Without a catch light, your subjects will look lifeless and considerably less attractive than if they had this tiny, but very important feature.

Often lighting conditions enable you to shoot with existing light and get a catch light. If you are shooting without the benefit of light that allows you to get a catch light, use a flash or other light source.

To avoid adding too much artificial light from a flash to your photo, use exposure compensation if it is available on your camera or flash to reduce the balance of light from the flash relative to existing light. The distance to the subject and the power of the flash are important variables to consider when setting flash exposure compensation. What you do not want to do is to ruin your intended natural lighting just to add catch light.

O This happy red-haired child's portrait was greatly enhanced with a flash to add a catch light to the eyes.

O This close-up photo shows the important catch light or sparkle light in the eyes of the red-haired child.

Prevent
RED EYE

#43

DIFFICULTY LEVEL

The dreaded *red eye* is caused by light from a flash reflected back from the subject's retina to the camera. Sadly, unnatural red eyes almost always ruin the resulting photograph. To avoid getting photographs whose subjects have red eyes, many camera vendors have added features that are known as red-eye reduction features. Although these features can reduce or eliminate red eye, they often create other problems. The best strategy is to learn how to shoot without using a red-eye reduction feature.

To avoid getting red eye, you simply need to shoot so that the angle between the flash and lens to the subject's eyes is more than 5 degrees. Using an off-camera flash is one way to avoid getting red eye. You can also have your subjects look away from the camera slightly, or find a shooting environment or use camera settings that do not require a flash. You are more likely to get red eye when shooting in a dark environment because the pupil will be wider and more prone to reflect red light.

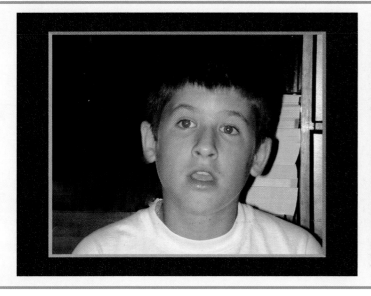

O This snapshot photo features the dreaded, all-too-common red eye caused by a flash.

O Red eye can even occur in the eyes of your pets and wildlife subjects, such as this great horned owl.

ADD NATURAL LIGHT
with a reflector

One useful and inexpensive photographic accessory is a light reflector such as the 32" Stroboframe Pops Portable Light Modifier, which costs under $35. You can use it to reflect soft natural light toward your subject and as a shade cover to reduce overly bright and high contrast direct sunlight. Most similar portable light reflectors fold up to ⅓ of their open size and they usually offer a white side and a second colored side such as silver, gold, or bronze.

A handheld light reflector is especially useful for adding light to a subject's face for a portrait. Besides filling shadows with natural light, you can add a warm color tone by using a bronze- or gold-colored reflector. When shooting a back-lit subject, a reflective light modifier such as the Stroboframe Light Modifier is an excellent tool to use to add natural "fill light" to the subject to reveal detail.

The Stroboframe Light Modifiers and similar products are available in multiple sizes and are easy to pack and carry in the field.

O This portrait was taken in bright direct sun with a Stroboframe Light Modifier to reduce contrast and to evenly light the face. Notice the absence of harsh shadows.

O An assistant is shown holding a Stroboframe Light Modifier to reflect light up towards the face of the model.

Did You Know? ※

Large white matte boards, which can be purchased at most art stores, make excellent inexpensive light reflectors. Although they are not as convenient to store and carry as the collapsible light modifiers such as the Stroboframe Pops Light Modifier shown below, they can be used to reflect light where it is needed. One advantage to using a reflector over an additional light source is that it will not alter the light's qualities causing problems with color temperature or shadows.

Apply It! ※

If you have only a single strobe or hot light when you need to have light coming from a second direction, you can use a reflector to bounce light back from the flash to the subject. Just place a reflector such as a Stroboframe Light Modifier or a white matte board opposite the light and reflect the light back to the subject to get an evenly-lit subject.

DIFFICULTY LEVEL

○ This wildflower photograph was taken on a bright sunny day under the shade created by a Stroboframe Light Modifier.

○ The photographer is using a self-timer and a Stroboframe Light Modifier to shade and photograph a wildflower without an assistant.

SHOOT CLOSE-UPS
with a macro ring light

If you are serious about taking close-up or macro photographs, you should consider getting a *macro ring light.* A macro ring light is a flash that attaches to and wraps around the front of a macro lens. Although it can light up shadows in such a way that the subject loses some definition, a skilled photographer can alter the ration of the light coming from the two lights to maintain realistic shadows. Most macro ring lights also have a modeling light that is useful for both seeing your subject and for providing enough light for your camera to auto-focus. Besides adding light to a subject, a macro ring light is extremely valuable for increasing depth of field. Whenever you shoot close to a subject, you have a limited depth of field. To maximize depth of field, you need to choose a small aperture, which means that you will have a long exposure. Long exposures allow small movements in the subject to record as a blurred subject. Using a flash, you can freeze the subject movement while benefiting from the increased depth of field, resulting in perfectly focused and exposed subjects.

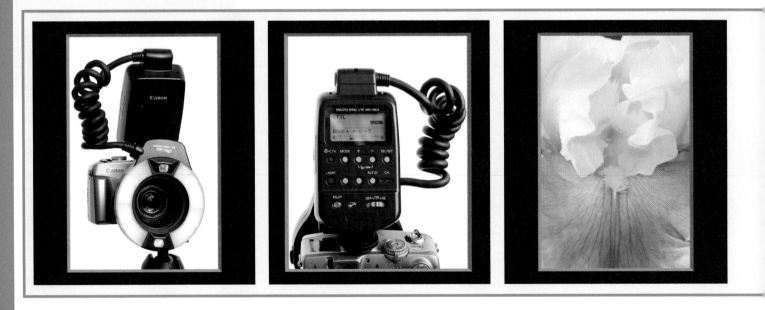

O A Canon MR-14EX TTL Macro Ring Lite Flash mounted on the front of a Canon PowerShot G2.

O The Canon MR-14EX TTL Macro Ring Lite Flash offers many features and control for taking well-lit photos.

O The interior details of this blue and yellow iris are well lit by a macro-ring light.

Did You Know? ※

When you shoot close-up or macro photographs, you should use a tripod. A tripod helps you accurately focus your photographs and more precisely control the depth-of-field and the composition.

Caution! ※

Vendors other than the major camera vendors make several excellent macro ring lights. However, be careful if you decide to purchase a macro ring light manufactured by a vendor other than the one that made your camera. You may not be able to use all the features. A good, but more expensive, option is to buy one from your camera manufacturer.

O A macro ring-light provided excellent light for this spider with catch light in the eyes.

O This close-up shot even shows detail in the cornea of the eyes of a turtle. It would have been difficult to light without a macro ring light.

Illuminate portraits with
WINDOW LIGHT

Getting a good portrait is highly dependent on the quality and quantity of light that is available. That is one of the reasons why so many portrait photographers strongly prefer to shoot inside a photography studio where they have the most control over lighting. One of the most useful lighting accessories in a portrait studio is a *soft box*, which is a large light box that diffuses the light from a flash to make soft, even, natural-looking light for well-lit portraits.

You can get the same soft, evenly diffused light in your own home without the expense of having a studio with studio flash and soft boxes by shooting portraits with the subject standing in front of a window.

Depending on the light, you can either shoot with the light coming in directly through the window, or you can use the diffused light that comes through a white sheer drape. If you want to control the background, you can have your subject hold a matte board up behind them as shown below.

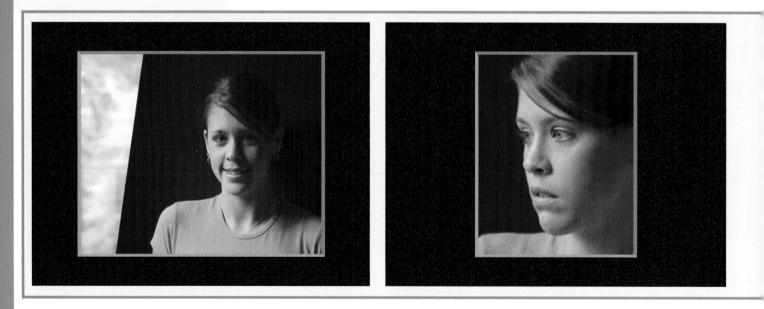

O You can create an excellent portrait by positioning your subject in front of a window while holding a matte board behind them as a background.

O A portrait taken using natural light shining in through a window.

Take advantage of the GOLDEN HOUR

The best sunlight is often found an hour or less before sunset to twenty minutes or so past sunset. This time is often referred to as the *golden hour* for photographers. Having the light low in the sky gives you a very directional light that adds wonderful depth to your photographs because of the shadows and directional light. The evening light is also usually warmer and richer in color than early morning light. If you shoot landscape photos, this is often a time you will rarely want to miss.

When you plan on taking advantage of the sun in the golden hour, be well prepared to shoot quickly, because the best of that time may come and go in just a few minutes. Make sure you have all your equipment out, set up, and ready to shoot, or you will have to wait for the next sunset. You should also wait twenty minutes past sunset for any possible *after-glow*, which occasionally makes for a spectacular landscape photograph, so do not pack up and leave too soon.

DIFFICULTY LEVEL

○ The golden hour of sunset casts a wonderful color on these reeds near the edge of the water.

○ Near-sunset light provides the rich warm color and black shadows shown in this forest.

○ The golden light from the evening sun makes a wonderful color for photographing this child playing with sticks.

CHAPTER 6

Creative Photo Ideas

Although you can take snapshots to document the events around you, the finer form of photography is all about having a vision of a photo you want, and then being able to use your camera to capture that vision. In order to develop your vision and increase your ability to effectively use your camera to capture it, you need to experiment and try different ideas. The more you shoot, experiment, and study your work and the work of others, the better your photography will be.

Coming up with creative photo ideas is easy and you will often be pleased with your results. In addition to trying ideas that are presented in photography books, you should also think of new ideas yourself.

For example, you can experiment with different features on your camera and use them creatively. Push each of the available settings to the extreme to see what results you get. Maximum and minimum aperture settings, and low shutter speeds are just two settings that can help you to get exciting photographs. Also, you should think about how to make various design elements more pronounced. Think of ways to shoot that put focus on the subject, capture bold or subtle colors, reveal patterns or shapes in complex scenes, or just shoot to capture elements or backgrounds to later combine with other images. The more you think about how to shoot creatively, the more you will understand how to shoot well!

TOP 100

FOCUS ATTENTION
on the subject

There are many ways you can focus attention on the subject. Color, texture, backgrounds, focus, perspective, and a wide range of visual design elements are just a few of the factors you can use to draw attention toward the subject.

The next time you shoot, think carefully about how you can focus more attention on the subject. Can you use a telephoto lens to fill the frame with the subject, or can you use a wide-angle lens to show a huge expanse of open space with a tiny subject that draws a viewer's attention? Maybe you can use a "new" vantage point where you look up at a subject that you ordinarily would look down at.

When using a long telephoto lens, you have considerable control over the depth of field, which enables you to show a sharply focused subject against a soft, blurred background with contrasting colors. Whatever strategy you use, placing more attention on your subject often results in a better photograph.

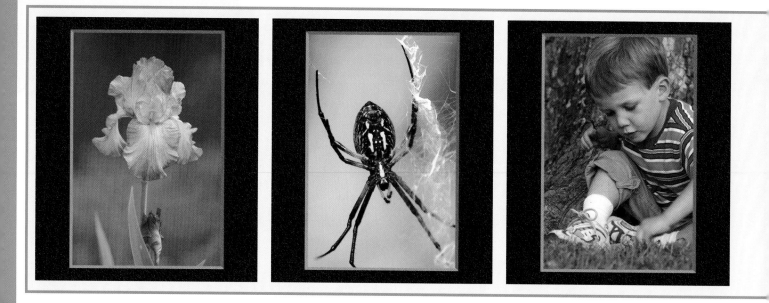

O A long telephoto lens and a large aperture were used to make this purple iris stand out against a blurred background.

O The bright green background from softly blurred plants helps focus attention on the spider on a web.

O The camera was positioned a few inches up from the ground to focus attention on the boy's activity.

#48

Photo Tip! ☀

You can use a telephoto lens to isolate a subject from its background because of its shallow depth of field and because it enables a photographer to fill the frame with a subject. When you want to isolate a subject with a telephoto lens, use an aperture setting that keeps your subject in focus, but creates a soft background. See tasks 32, 33, and 35 for more about focal length and depth of field.

Photo Tip! ☀

Sometimes the best way to focus attention on a subject is to keep your composition as simple as it can be. This strategy helps to minimize the number of distracting elements that can compete with the main subject.

○ Bright contrasting orange flowers isolate the yellow butterfly from the background.

○ Part of a walkway attached to the building frames this high-rise office tower.

○ The face of this lacrosse player was shot to fill the frame to keep attention on his gaze toward the field.

Shoot color for
DRAMATIC PHOTOS

Color can be one of the most powerful elements in a photograph. Certain colors evoke emotions and create moods; others are less apt to be noticed. Red, for example, is a color that is always quickly noticed, even when it takes up a small part of a photo. Most scenes or subjects can become spectacular or relatively uninteresting depending on the color of the light that is available. Study colors to learn how they work together and how they can be combined to ruin a photo. Although heavily saturated bold colors can be dramatic, so can soft, subtle colors and even scenes with little color that result in a monochromatic photograph.

When you find a subject or scene you like, visit and shoot it at different times of day over a few days to see how different light changes the colors. Your repeated visits will help you learn how to capture color as you want it. Shooting subjects slightly out of focus and underexposing sometimes can further enhance your photos to produce rich, saturated color.

O Richly saturated yellows, greens, and purples draws a viewers' attention to the iris.

O The quality of the soft pastel colors along with the soft focus effect help add interest to this water lily.

O The contrasting bright red vine leaves make this mostly monochromatic bark texture more interesting.

DIFFICULTY LEVEL

Did You Know? ☀

Color can sometimes say more
in a photograph than the subject.
Bold contrasting colors that are
balanced on a page will give the viewer an
entirely different impression than if the colors
are not balanced and cause some tension.

Did You Know? ☀

Some colors are more appealing than others.
One of the reasons that the time just before,
and shortly after, sunset is known as the
"golden hour" is that the rich warm golden light
bathes subjects in a very attractive rich warm
color. In contrast, colors in the blue family
illuminate scenes in a dull, "cool" manner.

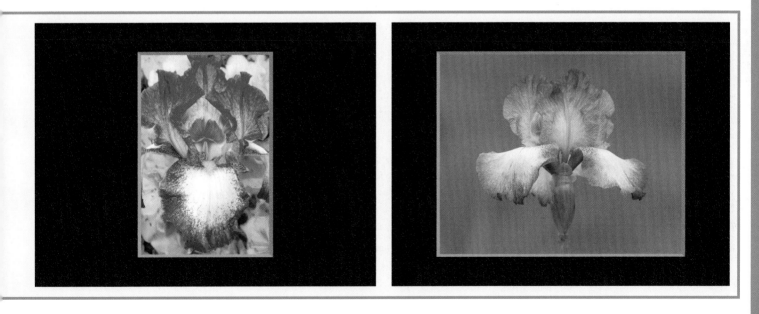

○ The pink flowers in the background help to clearly delineate the edges of the white and blue iris in the center of this photo.

○ The awful combination of the olive green background against the purple and white iris shows how important it is to shoot to capture colors that work well together.

Show movement with a
NEUTRAL DENSITY FILTER

You can use a slow shutter speed to show movement by recording a moving subject as being partly blurred. However, sometimes you cannot choose a slow enough shutter speed when shooting in bright light, because cameras have a limit to the minimum size of aperture opening. That limit may require a shutter speed that is too fast to show motion. In such cases, you can use a *neutral density* filter to reduce shutter speed by one or more stops.

A neutral density filter is nothing more than a glass lens filter that reduces the amount of light that gets to the image sensor in your digital camera without having any effect on color. Neutral density filters are usually rated as 2X, 4X, and 8X, and they decrease the light by 1, 2, and 3 stops, respectively. Generally, when you use a neutral density filter and a slow shutter speed to show motion, you will need to use a tripod.

To learn more about showing motion in your photos, see task #29 and task #30.

O A combination of the shade from a tree and a neutral density filter allows a slow-enough shutter speed to be used to capture the motion of this person walking and gives her a ghost-like appearance.

O Without the use of a neutral density filter, this photo of a motorcycle could not have been taken because there was too much light to use a slow enough shutter speed to create this panning effect.

Control reflection with a
POLARIZER

A *polarizer* is a filter that attaches to your lens. Polarizers have two primary uses: to remove light reflections and to enhance or deepen color saturation. When used to increase color saturation, you must shoot at a right angle to the sun. As you turn more toward or away from a right angle to the sun, you are able to control less of the effect. *Circular* polarizers can be rotated, which allows you to control the level of effect. When you use a polarizer to enhance colors, you need to be careful to not overuse

the effect, as it can result in a contrasty and wholly unacceptable photo.

When you want to shoot without the distraction from light reflections, you can use a polarizer to reduce or eliminate them all together. A polarizer is useful, for example, when you want to shoot through a glass window and show what is inside, or to shoot toward water and show what is beneath the surface. You can also use a polarizer to control bright reflections from reflective or shiny surfaces like metal or glass.

DIFFICULTY LEVEL

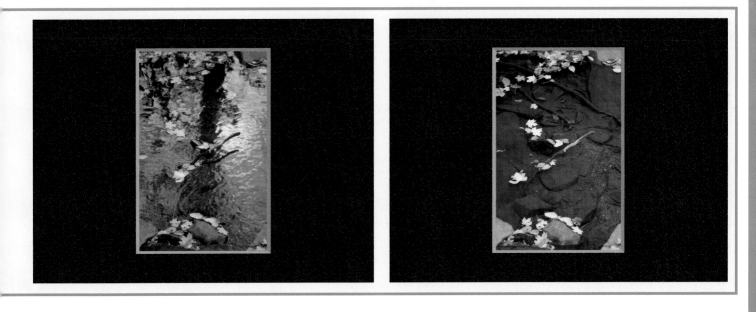

○ Reflections of saturated colors of the trees and sky make the bottom of this shallow stream hard to see.

○ A polarizer filter removed the reflections so that the bottom of the stream is now visible.

Shoot photos for a
PANORAMA

As long as photographs have been taken, it has always been a challenge for photographers to capture the beauty found in wide-sweeping scenes. A wide-angle lens can capture more of a scene than a shorter focal length lens, but wide-angle lenses tend to add unwanted distortion to the photos and they still do not capture as much of a scene as is often desired. Using one of the digital stitching applications or a feature like Adobe Photoshop Elements' Photomerge, you can shoot and later combine multiple photos into a single, long vertical or horizontal panoramic photo.

When you shoot photos that you will later combine using a digital stitching application, you need to overlap each photo by 1/3 to 1/2 so that you can match and blend the images seamlessly. You also need to be careful to maintain the same exposure throughout your photos. Avoid shooting moving subjects such as clouds or ocean waves that make photos too different to be combined. Finally, you should always use a tripod.

O These four photographs of a country landscape were taken with a camera mounted on a tripod with a head that allows panning.

Did You Know? ※

You can use Adobe Photoshop Element's Photomerge feature to combine multiple photos into a single, large photo for making large prints. If your digital camera does not have enough pixels to make a quality print in the size you want, you can shoot several photos and combine them with Photomerge.

Did You Know? ※

You can take multiple photos of vertical subjects and create vertical panoramas as easily as you can create horizontal panoramas. Good subjects for vertical panoramas include tall trees or buildings. Shooting from a distance with a telephoto lens can help minimize unwanted perspective distortion caused by using lenses with shorter focal lengths.

O This photo was created by digitally stitching together the four photos shown on the prior page. Adobe Photoshop Elements was used to stitch the images together and to make additional edits like the color change.

Shoot photos with a
WOW!
factor

No matter what subjects you like to shoot, there are times where you can capture a photo with a "Wow!" factor. If you shoot sports photos, it may be a photo of two soccer players up in the air heading a ball at the same time, showing the intensity of the play with sweat flying off their faces as you capture the perfect moment where the ball is compressed between their heads.

Nature photographers are always looking to photograph elk with record-setting antlers, or the perfect red fox in golden light, or maybe a black bear mother with four cubs (a rare occurrence). To get photographs with a "Wow!" factor, you need to look for exceptional light, perfect natural specimens, unusual occurrences, or maybe you just get enough of the photographic variables correct that you get an outstanding photograph through good vision, camera settings, and composition. Often the trick to getting a photo with a high "Wow!" factor is being in the right place at the right time and then using your skills to capture the perfect shot.

DIFFICULTY LEVEL

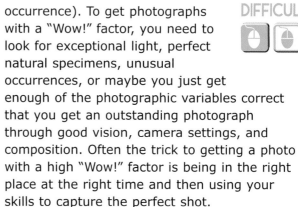

○ A row of Black-Necked Stilts fishing together as a team is as amazing to watch as it is to see in a photo.

○ Wow! What's this foot attached to? Sometimes it is what is not in a photo that makes it interesting.

○ Thousands of wintering birds flying and grazing in open fields can be an awesome thing to see, hear, and photograph.

Shoot scenes with
LOW CONTRAST

DIFFICULTY LEVEL

Soft diffused light tends to reduce contrast and can be used to produce wonderful photographs. Unlike bright light that can create more contrast than you can captured on an image sensor or film, soft light enables you to show good detail in all parts of an image and allows you to get wonderful smooth gradations that can make superb photographs.

Learn to look for low-contrast light and take advantage of it when you find it. Early-morning or late-evening light is usually a good time to find low-contrast light with good color. Mist, fog, haze, or clouds can also create excellent low-contrast light that is a joy to shoot. Besides reducing contrast, these lighting conditions can also reduce color saturation and enable you to capture monochromatic images that can be simple and powerful.

Finding low-contrast light is not always easy. Some geographic areas rarely have anything but brightly lit skies, and other places are known for rarely having direct sunlight. Being able to shoot low-contrast light is often a matter of place, time, and chance.

O The light remaining after the sun dropped below the horizon made the warm glowing colors behind this silhouetted coastline.

O Low light levels help create the smooth two-toned gradation that is the background for this digitally edited tree.

O The low-contrast light that creates the wonderful two-toned gradation enhances this simple photograph of a coastal waterway.

Shoot when SEASONS CHANGE

You can usually get out-of-the-ordinary photos by shooting when the seasons change. In early spring you can find new buds that can be fascinating to watch as they open. Spring can also bring a nice contrast between the dark browns of winter plants and the green colors of the new spring plants.

Undoubtedly, the rich bold colors of fall can also be key factors for getting extraordinary photos that are hard to match when shooting at any other time of the year. Determining the exact time to get the best fall colors and when various plants and trees bloom is more a matter of chance than planning. The best approach for deciding when to go to shoot fall colors is to watch them yourself, or find someone who can give you a daily update if you live too far away to visit except when shooting. These wonderful and rather short periods between seasons can provide you with some of the best photographic opportunities of the year.

O Careful observation of nature in early spring can be both helpful in providing you a deeper understanding of your subjects.

O The sweet gum tree grows new buds and these inedible spiny fruits, which hang for a few weeks before dropping.

O The opening of a bud on many plants and trees can be amazing to watch and photograph over a few days.

Shoot PATTERNS AND SHAPES

DIFFICULTY LEVEL

As a photographer, you can choose from many elements to draw attention to your photographs. Patterns and shapes can often become the strongest elements in a photograph, and you can find them everywhere after you develop a skill for noticing them and capturing them with your camera.

Our minds are always working to make sense of what the eyes see by looking for patterns and shapes in the complex and often over-cluttered environment we live in. The result is that patterns and shapes are pleasing. Patterns are formed by the repetition of objects, shapes, lines,

or colors. Sometimes it is the pattern or shape that makes a photograph a good one, rather than the subject itself. In fact, many good photographs feature a strong pattern or shape that is made by something that is not even recognizable.

When you find a pattern or shape, think how you should shoot it to make an interesting photograph. Use light to make a silhouette, or maybe even use bright highlights to strengthen the patterns or shape.

O The softly focused lupine in the background mirrors the graceful shape of the blue lupine flower.

O The shapes and the orientation of the blurred grasses behind it further enhance this single elegant yellow fern's shape.

O The shape and color of this brightly colored wildflower adds interest to this photograph.

SHOOT WITH A PLAN
to edit digitally

After you start taking photos with a digital camera and editing them with an image editor, you have moved into an entirely new world of possibilities. Each time you shoot, you should be thinking about what it is you can or cannot do with your image editor after you have taken a photograph; otherwise you will be vastly limiting what it is you can create photographically.

Because you can combine one or more photos or parts of a photo, remove unwanted parts, substantially modify contrast and tonal range, and much more, you need to think carefully about what you decide to shoot, how you shoot, and even what you may not want to shoot. In the past, because of the cost of film, you may have avoided taking a landscape photo that featured a telephone line or maybe a car that ruined the photo. Or maybe you avoided taking a photo because the contrast was too extreme. When you shoot and edit digitally, you can frequently correct these problems with an image editor.

O This photo of a field of wildflowers was intentionally blurred so that it could be combined with the photo on the right to get a soft-focus, double-exposure effect.

O This photo was taken to add to the photo on the left as a layer with a blend mode in an image editor.

#57

Photo Tip! ☀

Think about and shoot photo objects and backgrounds. The next time you find a wonderful subject like an old car sitting in field with an ugly bright sky, think photo object. Then, when you find a perfect background scene for that car, shoot it and combine it with the old car and foreground.

Did You Know? ☀

You should *always* work to take the best photo that you can when shooting. Many photographers new to digital photo editing believe that they can "fix" anything wrong with a photo after they have taken it. That is not always the case. You will *always* end up with a better photo after editing it, if you first start with an excellent photo.

○ Digital brush strokes and filter effects transformed this photo of the Sedona desert into a digital painting.

○ A pelican was shot specifically to become an object to be used in another photo, like this one of a swing in the woods.

○ A plain wall in a New Mexico canyon covered in bright sunlight was photographed with a vision to use an image editor to make this more-interesting photo.

Experiment to create
UNIQUE PHOTOS

Break all the photography rules and guidelines you know. Shoot with a slow shutter speed without a tripod. Zoom or pan your lens with the shutter open while shooting with a slow shutter speed. Intentionally overexpose and underexpose, shoot in high-contrast light, shoot in low light, shoot in the rain or a snow storm. Shoot a subject that you ordinarily do not shoot. Take 50 photos while shooting from ground level. Take 50 photos with your camera set to the smallest aperture. Shoot using extremes — extreme vantage points, extreme focal lengths, extreme aperture settings, and extreme distances to the subject.

When you shoot a popularly photographed subject or scene, think carefully about all the obvious and common shots that are taken, and then try to come up with a dozen new ways to shoot the same subject or scene. Maybe you change the angle of view or the vantage point. Or shoot with a different light or shoot from a distance and frame the subject with some foreground element. Experimentation and carefully thinking about each photograph you take is always good.

DIFFICULTY LEVEL

O Using a slow shutter speed, the zoom lens was zoomed while the aperture was open to get this photo.

O Slight horizontal panning while the aperture was open created this blurred sunset effect.

O Attention is drawn to one book in this book store by zooming the lens with a slow shutter speed.

Shoot in low light for
RICH COLORS

#59

Long exposures in low-light environments can create rich glowing colors that can make spectacular photographs. City streets at night, building interiors, or nighttime reflections in windows can be good subjects to shoot. Fairgrounds with brightly lit moving rides can result in some spectacular images with the brightly colored lights represented as blurred streaks of heavily saturated colors.

When you shoot in low light levels, you will need to use a tripod to get sharply focused photographs. To minimize camera shake caused by pressing the camera's shutter release, you can further reduce any blur caused by camera

movement by using a timed shutter release feature if your camera has one or an optional cable shutter release.

Richly colored sunsets can provide wonderful light for taking photos with dramatic color. Instead of shooting toward the sunset, turn and shoot away from the sunset using the light coming from the sun to light subjects of interest to you. Or, you can use the light from brightly colored sunsets as backlight to get wonderful silhouettes with glowing backgrounds that outline the silhouetted subject.

DIFFICULTY LEVEL

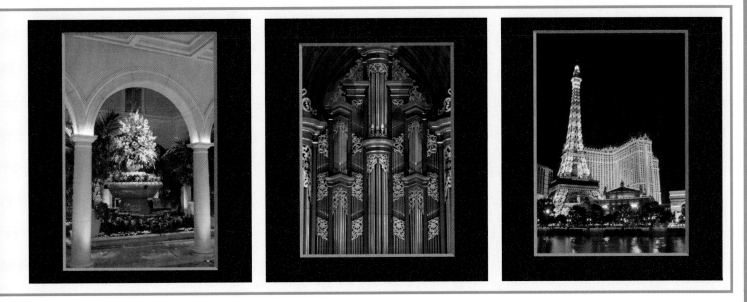

○ The vase of flowers shown through this archway are all illuminated in rich colors that were captured in low light with a tripod mounted camera.

○ These church organ pipes were hardly noticeable in the low light level, but they glowed in a photo taken with a camera mounted on a tripod using a long exposure.

○ The richly saturated colors of this Las Vegas hotel was captured using an exposure time of two seconds.

Edit Images with Adobe Photoshop Elements

After you have taken photos with your digital camera and have downloaded them to your computer, they are ready to be digitally edited. Using an image editor such as Adobe Photoshop Elements, you can substantially improve the quality of the image, plus transform or alter your digital photos in an almost infinite number of ways. This chapter requires familiarity with basic Photoshop Elements commands; to learn these commands or refresh your memory of them, see *Teach Yourself VISUALLY Restoration and Retouching with Photoshop Elements 2* (Wiley, 2003).

The first thing you should do before performing any edits is to evaluate each photo and make a plan.

Important questions include: Do the photos first need to be converted from the RAW format? How can you improve your digital photo in terms of color and overall tonal range and contrast? How else do you want to alter or fix the photos? Do you need to add or remove elements? How will you be using the edited images? Will they be used on a Web page, shared as an attachment to an e-mail, or made into a large print on an inkjet printer?

Only after you have answered these questions will you be able to effectively edit your photos to get the results you want. Learning when to save your image files to preserve your work and the quality of the image is also important.

TOP 100

Learn the best
EDITING SEQUENCE

The order of the steps you take to edit your digital photos matters. Anytime you perform edits on a digital photo, you alter some of the original picture data. Although the image may look better, you have less original picture information than you did when you first opened the image. So, the first step to take when editing an image is to save it under another filename so that you preserve the original "digital negative."

As you make various kinds of edits, you may find that you want to go back a few steps or change some of the settings used on an earlier step. You

can do this without degrading image quality if you use Undo History and adjustment layers. Also, you want to be sure to perform any steps for increasing image size or sharpening at the end, *after* you have already saved your file.

Proper image-editing workflow may result in many copies of each image in addition to the never-edited original and an archived backup copy of important originals and edited versions.

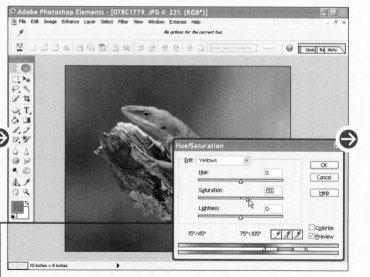

① Straighten, crop, adjust tonal range and contrast, and remove unwanted color casts.

② Perform any additional image edits as needed except for image resizing or sharpening.

#60

Did You Know? ※

No matter how you increase the size of a digital photo, the image quality decreases to some extent. Because of this, you should generally complete your edits on the original-sized image and only increase image size when you know the specifications of the print size and the target printer.

Did You Know? ※

The best image-sharpening settings to use when applying the Adobe Photoshop Elements Unsharp Mask are very dependent on the size of the image and how you are going to use it. For this reason, you should apply the Unsharp Mask only when you know how you are going to use the image and what size you need.

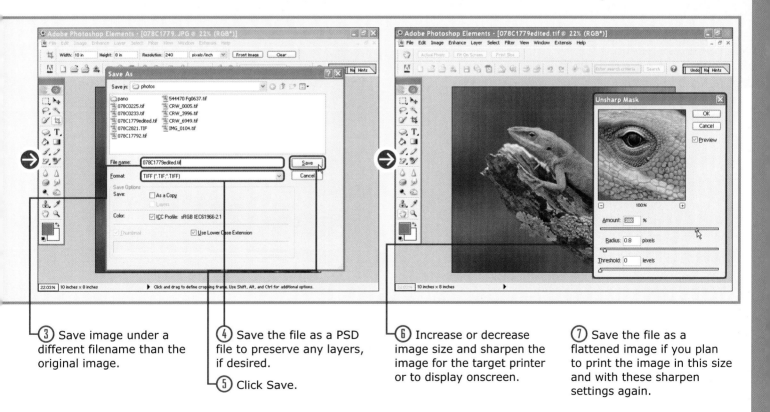

③ Save image under a different filename than the original image.

④ Save the file as a PSD file to preserve any layers, if desired.

⑤ Click Save.

⑥ Increase or decrease image size and sharpen the image for the target printer or to display onscreen.

⑦ Save the file as a flattened image if you plan to print the image in this size and with these sharpen settings again.

Convert RAW files with
ADOBE CAMERA RAW

You realize some of the most significant benefits of using a digital camera only if you shoot in the RAW format. When you use the RAW format, you save your image without applying many of the camera's settings, such as white balance. Not only does this mean that you no longer have to worry about using some of the wrong camera settings, but you have considerable control over how your picture looks *after* you take it.

As RAW files are proprietary to each camera vendor, differences exist between vendors and even specific camera models. You need to use a RAW image

converter that supports your camera model to get an image that you can edit. Before purchasing the Adobe Camera RAW Plug-in or any other RAW image file converter, make sure the software supports your camera model.

After you install the Adobe Camera RAW Plug-in, you can double-click RAW images in the Adobe Photoshop Elements File Browser to open them in the Adobe Camera RAW dialog box and convert them. To learn more about the RAW file format, see task #4.

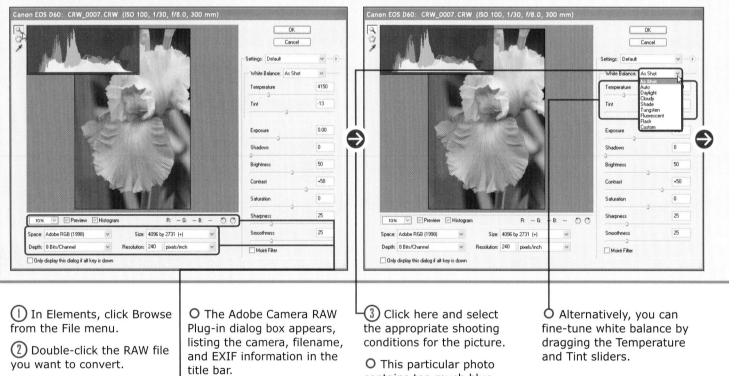

① In Elements, click Browse from the File menu.

② Double-click the RAW file you want to convert.

○ The Adobe Camera RAW Plug-in dialog box appears, listing the camera, filename, and EXIF information in the title bar.

○ These options control the image preview.

○ Image attributes display here.

③ Click here and select the appropriate shooting conditions for the picture.

○ This particular photo contains too much blue, giving the flower an unnatural purple appearance.

○ Alternatively, you can fine-tune white balance by dragging the Temperature and Tint sliders.

DIFFICULTY LEVEL

Did You Know? ☀

Camera vendors that sell digital cameras that support the RAW image format provide their own proprietary RAW image file converter software. However, generally, the converters that are included with the camera are remarkably inferior to those provided by third-party vendors. The most popular RAW converters are Adobe's Camera RAW Plug-in (www.adobe.com), Breeze Systems' BreezeBrowser (www.breezesys.com), Bibble Labs' Bibble (www.bibblelabs.com), and Phase One's Capture One DSLR (www.phaseone.com).

Did You Know? ☀

One disadvantage of using the RAW format is that it takes considerable computer processing power (and time) to convert RAW images. Also, you cannot view your RAW images as thumbnails in your thumbnail browser unless your camera's RAW files are supported.

④ Adjust other settings as desired.

○ This photo was underexposed and required an increased Exposure value.

○ The Exposure slider allows you to adjust exposure compensation or tonal adjustments without compressing the image or losing any of the original image data.

⑤ Click here and select the desired image size.

⑥ Click OK to apply your changes and close the dialog box.

○ Adobe Camera RAW opens the image in a new document window in Adobe Photoshop Elements.

Convert RAW files with
CAPTURE ONE DSLR LE

Phase One's Capture One DSLR Limited Edition is an image browser in addition to a RAW file converter. It creates super exceptional images. Even though Phase One's Capture One DSLR Limited Edition application is a standalone application, as opposed to being a plug-in, you can configure it to open converted images in the image editor of your choice.

Like all of the RAW image file converters, Capture One DSLR LE supports a limited set of RAW image files. Before purchasing this product or any other RAW converter, check to make sure that it supports your specific camera model.

Unlike most RAW image file converters, Capture One DSLR LE lets you browse and work on an image while conversion is taking place in the background. You can also choose settings for an image and see the changes in real time in the preview window. These settings are saved without having to take the time and disk space to save the file. This workflow-enhancing feature, along with many others, makes this an excellent application for converting large numbers of RAW files.

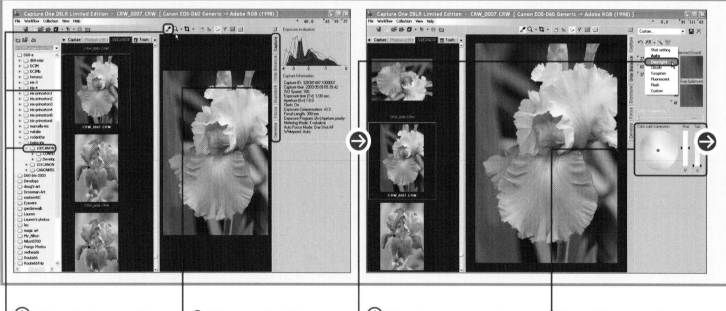

① Click a folder containing image files.

② Click the file you want to convert.

③ Click here to select the Eyedropper, Zoom, Crop, and other tools.

○ This photo's white balance may be improved.

○ Clicking a function tab selects that particular workflow step.

④ Click here and select a Color Balance setting.

○ Powerful color balance tools enable precise color correction.

62

Did You Know? ☀

Phase One's Capture One DSLR Limited Edition offers a subset of the features that are available in the full version of Capture One DSLR, but the LE version supports fewer camera models. Using the full version, you can work in tethered mode with your camera attached to your computer, allowing you to view camera settings and make adjustments as you shoot.

Did You Know? ☀

One of the advantages of shooting RAW image files and converting them with a RAW image file converter is that most RAW image file converters work in full bit depth. This means that edits are performed using all the picture data available from the camera, which ensures a higher quality image.

DIFFICULTY LEVEL

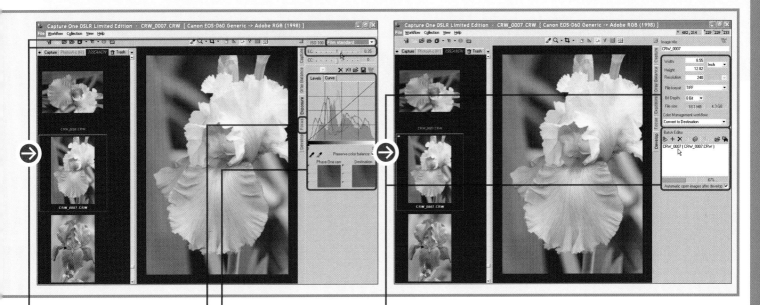

⑤ Click here and select a film curve to get optimal distribution of tonal range.

⑥ Drag the Exposure Compensation slider up to +/− two stops to correct exposure.

○ For precise tonal manipulation, you can use the Levels and Curves adjustment features.

○ The Focus tab provides tools to control image sharpness.

⑦ Specify the desired image size and resolution, file format, bit depth, and color profiles.

○ The Batch Editor allows you to specify where to save the converted files and if they should be opened in an image editor.

⑧ Click on the develop icon to save the file to a default folder and open the image in a new document window in the selected image editor.

Use the Clone Stamp Tool to
REMOVE UNWANTED ELEMENTS

You can remove a variety of unwanted elements from your photos using a few different tools found in Adobe Photoshop Elements. You can remove everything from unwanted telephone lines or vehicles in landscape photos to people or objects in group photos. Without question, some elements are easier to remove than others. Most often, the best approach is to replace the unwanted element with another part of the image. If this is possible, the quickest approach is to use the Clone Stamp tool to "clone" existing areas over the unwanted elements.

The Clone Stamp tool allows you to set a *source point* in the image you are editing, or even another image. After you set the source point, you can paint with the Clone Stamp tool to replace the unwanted element with the image from the source.

You can also cut and paste one part of an image into another part to cover unwanted elements if the source image fits in terms of texture, color, or subject.

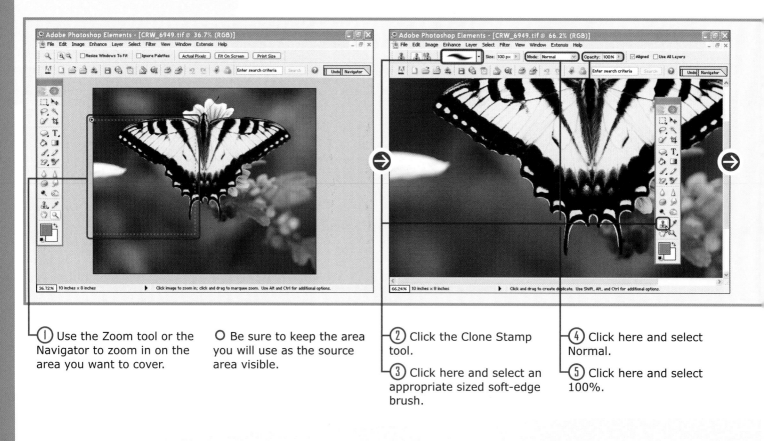

① Use the Zoom tool or the Navigator to zoom in on the area you want to cover.

○ Be sure to keep the area you will use as the source area visible.

② Click the Clone Stamp tool.

③ Click here and select an appropriate sized soft-edge brush.

④ Click here and select Normal.

⑤ Click here and select 100%.

Did You Know? ※

When you have a limited source area that can be used to replace an unwanted element, you can try adjusting the opacity to add some variation to the area you are painting. Then you can use the newly created area to use as a source for the remaining area that needs to be replaced.

Did You Know? ※

You can also use the Clone Stamp tool to add another element to an image. For example, if you take a family portrait that is missing one or more people, you can paint-in the missing people by setting the source point to the people you need from another photograph.

63

DIFFICULTY LEVEL

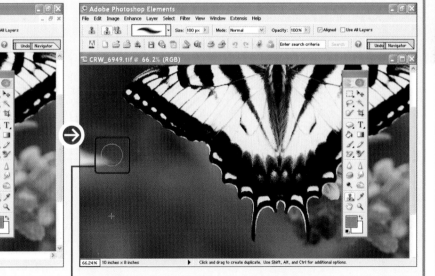

⑥ While holding down the Alt (Option) key, click on the photo to set the source point.

⑦ Click on the photo over the unwanted element.

O The Clone Stamp tool paints over the unwanted element.

O Click often while painting so that you can easily remove any unwanted brush strokes with Ctrl+Z (Command+Z).

Edit a
SELECTED AREA

Sometimes you may want to perform *selective edits,* which occur when you apply a filter or make edits to only a portion of the image instead of the entire image. To perform a selective edit, you must first select the area you want to edit. Adobe Photoshop Elements offers many different tools for selecting parts of an image. Depending on the characteristics of the area you want to select, one tool may be more appropriate than another. Or, you may want to use more than one tool and keep adding to a selected area until you have selected all of the desired area.

Good tools for selecting parts of an image include the Rectangular and Elliptical Marquee tools, the Lasso tool, the Magic Wand tool, and the Selection Brush tool. Some of these tools allow you to select parts of an image at a time and keep adding to the selection. Some tools, such as the Rectangular and Elliptical tools, also allow you to subtract from the selection by changing the selection mode in the Tool options bar.

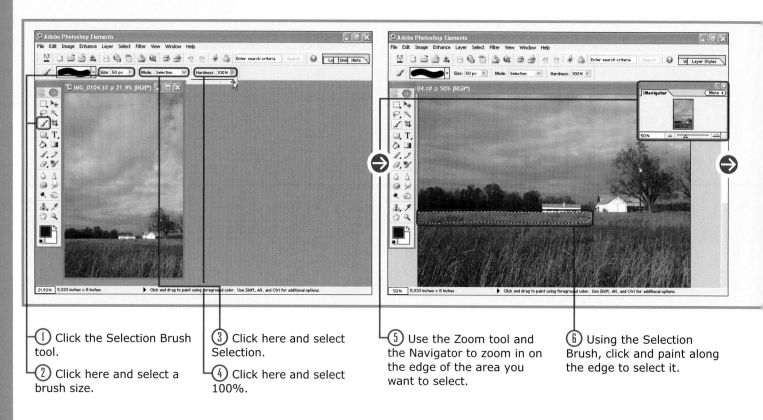

① Click the Selection Brush tool.

② Click here and select a brush size.

③ Click here and select Selection.

④ Click here and select 100%.

⑤ Use the Zoom tool and the Navigator to zoom in on the edge of the area you want to select.

⑥ Using the Selection Brush, click and paint along the edge to select it.

64

DIFFICULTY LEVEL

Did You Know? ✷

One of the challenges in selecting complex areas to edit independently of the rest of the images is to not loose your selection. If you think you may need to perform additional editing on a selected area, you can copy and paste it into the image as a new layer. However, if you do this, you will not be able to make global edits to the entire image unless you flatten the layer.

Did You Know? ✷

When making selections with the Selection Brush tool, you should click and paint in small strokes, which enables you to step back one stroke using Ctrl+Z (Command+Z) when you paint outside the intended area, thereby saving you from having to redo the entire selection.

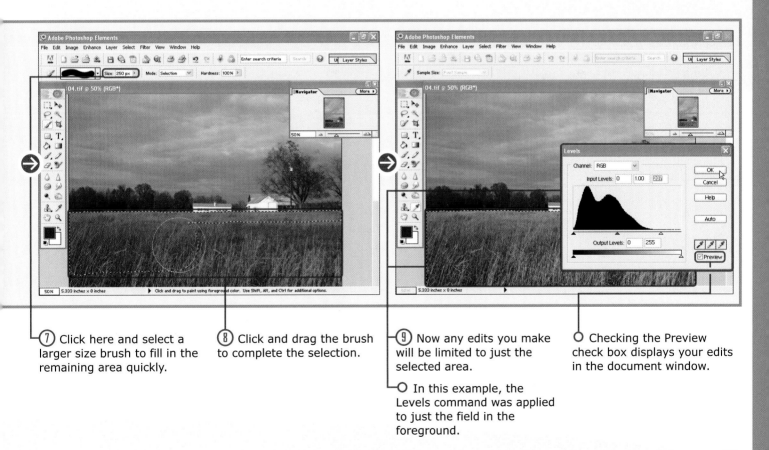

⑦ Click here and select a larger size brush to fill in the remaining area quickly.

⑧ Click and drag the brush to complete the selection.

⑨ Now any edits you make will be limited to just the selected area.

○ In this example, the Levels command was applied to just the field in the foreground.

○ Checking the Preview check box displays your edits in the document window.

KEEP TRACK
of your edits

Editing digital images is often a process of trial and error. You make a few edits and then decide if you like the results. If you do not like the results, the Undo History palette makes it easy to back up one or more steps. The Undo History palette keeps track of all the steps, which are called *history states.* When you exceed the maximum number of history states set in Preferences, Elements deletes the earliest history state each time you add a new one.

Using the Undo History palette, you can back up one or more steps and then move forward again by clicking each step in the Undo History palette while comparing the results. When you back up one or more steps and then make a new edit, however, Elements discards all steps from that point on as you add each new edit to the palette. You can also delete a history state by clicking it in the Undo History palette and then dragging it onto the Trash button at the bottom of the palette.

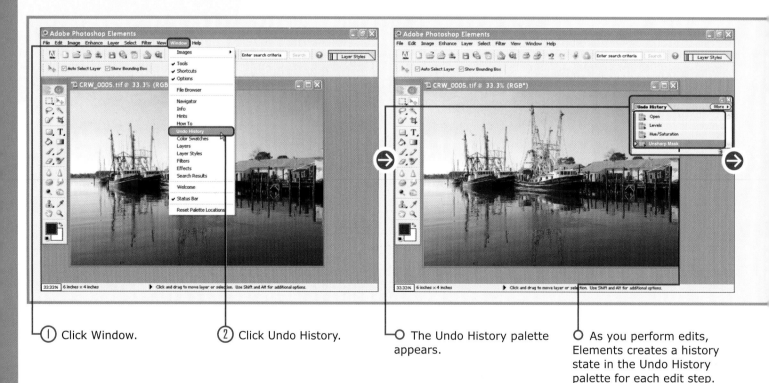

① Click Window.

② Click Undo History.

○ The Undo History palette appears.

○ As you perform edits, Elements creates a history state in the Undo History palette for each edit step.

Did You Know? ☀

When working on a large
image, it can take considerable
memory to maintain a long list of
history states in the Undo History
palette. You can increase or decrease
the amount of Undo states that are saved
by changing the value in the History States
box in the General Preferences dialog box. The
default value is 20.

Did You Know? ☀

You can back up one or more states in the Undo History
palette without using the palette by simply pressing
Ctrl+Z (Command+Z), which is the shortcut keystroke
for Step Backwards. If you want to go all the way back
in history to the last saved file, you can do so by
choosing the File menu and then Revert.

ᵗᵗ65

DIFFICULTY LEVEL

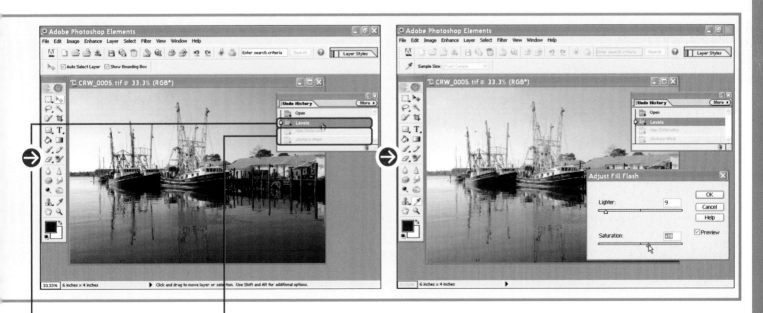

③ Click a previous history
state at which you want to
view the image or begin
making new edits.

○ History states occurring
after the selected state are
"ghosted" until you add a
new step, in which case they
disappear.

○ If you want to edit from
that point on, perform the
next edit and the Undo
History palette will reflect
the new edit history.

○ For example, the Adjust
Fill Flash command was
applied instead of Levels.

Test retouching and restoring edits using ADJUSTMENT LAYERS

CLONE TOOL

Whenever you apply the Levels, Brightness/Contrast, Hue/Saturation, Gradient Map, Invert, Threshold, or Posterize command, you make permanent changes to the image. You cannot go back and make minor adjustments to the settings of any one of these commands unless you step all the way back in the editing process using the Undo History palette. Then, if you change settings, you will lose all the steps following that step. However, if you use an adjustment layer when you apply any of those seven commands, you can always return to that layer and make changes to the settings. This is such a

powerful feature that it is usually wise to use adjustment layers when you apply any of the seven filters.

To create an adjustment layer, choose Layer, New Adjustment Layer, and then pick one of the seven different types of adjustment layers to suit your needs. After creating a new layer, you can name it and the adjustment layer shows up in the Layers palette.

See task #65 to learn more about tracking your edits using the Undo History palette.

① Click Window and then Layers if the Layers palette is not showing.

② Choose Layer.

③ Choose New Adjustment Layer.

④ Choose Hue/Saturation to create a Hue/Saturation Adjustment Layer.

○ The Hue/Saturation dialog box appears.

⑤ Specify the settings you want.

⑥ Click OK to apply the settings.

○ You can add one or more adjustment layers or one or more edit steps.

#66

DIFFICULTY LEVEL

Did You Know? ※

You can turn on or turn off the effects of one or more adjustment layers by clicking on the Layer Visibility (eye) icon at the far left of each adjustment layer in the Layers palette.

Did You Know? ※

When you are sure that you will not need to make any further changes to an Adjustment Layer, you can flatten your image to reduce the file size of your image. Click the layer you no longer need to make it the active layer. Then click the More button in the upper-right corner of the Layers palette to get a pop-up menu. Choose Merge Down to flatten one layer, or choose Flatten Image to flatten all layers in the Layers palette.

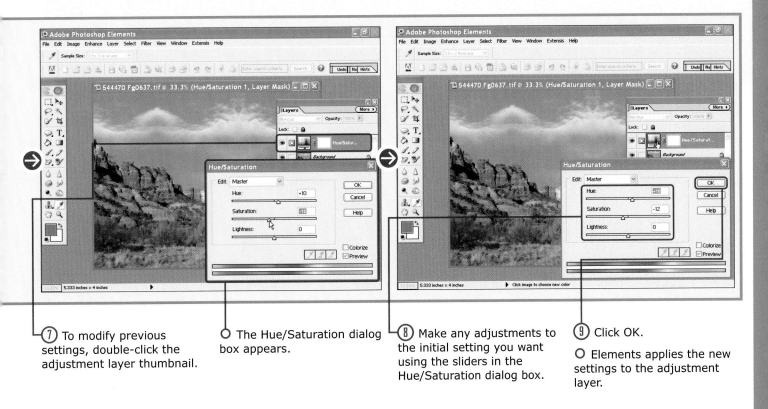

⑦ To modify previous settings, double-click the adjustment layer thumbnail.

○ The Hue/Saturation dialog box appears.

⑧ Make any adjustments to the initial setting you want using the sliders in the Hue/Saturation dialog box.

⑨ Click OK.

○ Elements applies the new settings to the adjustment layer.

CLONE TOOL

Create a
PANORAMA

As long as photographs have been taken, it has always been a challenge for photographers to capture the beauty found in wide-sweeping outdoor scenes. Wide-angle lenses can capture more of a scene than shorter focal length lenses, but wide-angle lenses tend to add unwanted distortion to the photos and they still do not capture as much of a scene that is often desired. Using one of the "digital stitching" applications or a feature like Adobe

Photoshop Elements' Photomerge, you can shoot and later combine multiple photos into a single long vertical or horizontal panoramic photo.

Task #52 shows how to take photographs that you can later digitally stitch into one panoramic print. If you have taken your own pictures for such a purpose, you are ready to use the Photomerge command in Adobe Photoshop Elements to do the stitching.

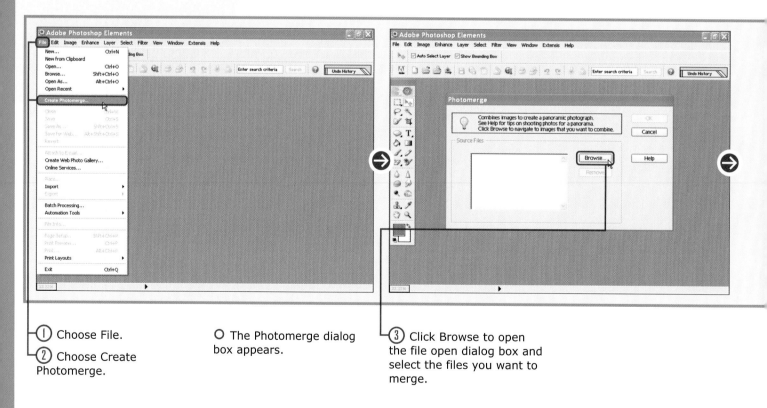

① Choose File.

② Choose Create Photomerge.

○ The Photomerge dialog box appears.

③ Click Browse to open the file open dialog box and select the files you want to merge.

#67

Photo Tip!

You can use Adobe Photoshop Element's Photomerge feature to combine multiple photos into a single large photo for making large prints. If your digital camera does not have enough pixels to make a quality print in the size you want, you can shoot several photos and combine them with Photomerge.

Did You Know?

You can take multiple photos of vertical subjects and create vertical panoramas as easily as you can create horizontal panoramas. Good subjects for vertical panoramas include tall trees or buildings. Shooting from a distance with a telephoto lens helps minimize unwanted perspective distortion caused by using shorter focal length lenses.

CONTINUED ▶

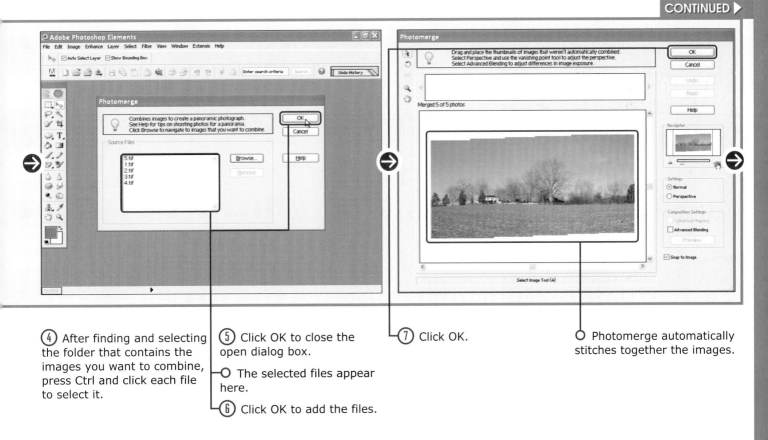

④ After finding and selecting the folder that contains the images you want to combine, press Ctrl and click each file to select it.

⑤ Click OK to close the open dialog box.

○ The selected files appear here.

⑥ Click OK to add the files.

⑦ Click OK.

○ Photomerge automatically stitches together the images.

Create a
PANORAMA

On rare occasions, Photomerge will not be able to automatically align your digital photos. When that occurs, you will see the photos placed in a window at the top off the Photomerge dialog box. To align the images, simply drag and place the images that were not automatically aligned. When you get the images close to where they should be, Photomerge should be able to automatically and precisely position them.

If you want to create more perspective than is visible in the combined images, you can place a

check mark in the Perspective box and then click once in the image to select the vanishing point. Photomerge adds some perspective to the combined image. If you use the perspective feature, it is important to have up to a 50 percent overlap in the photos you are using; otherwise gaps may occur between each image at the top and bottom of the combined images. Placing a check mark in the Advanced Blending mode box results in a more seamless blend between each image.

CONTINUED ▶

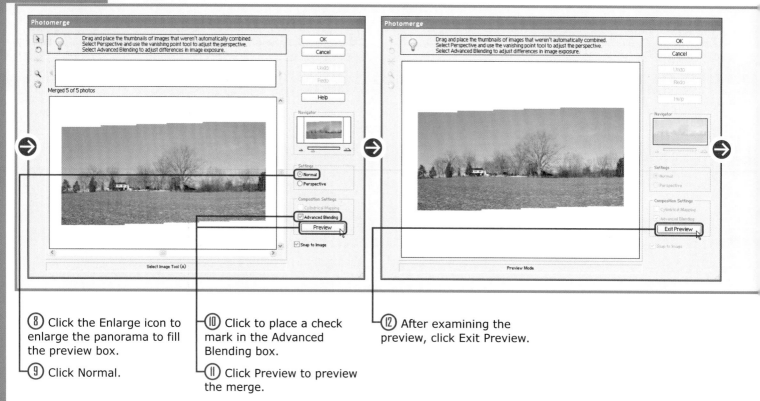

⑧ Click the Enlarge icon to enlarge the panorama to fill the preview box.

⑨ Click Normal.

⑩ Click to place a check mark in the Advanced Blending box.

⑪ Click Preview to preview the merge.

⑫ After examining the preview, click Exit Preview.

Did You Know? ※

Some digital photo-stitching applications allow you to shoot a series of pictures that cover a full 360-degree view. You can then combine these images into a video that you can move to the left and right by clicking the image and dragging it in the direction you want it to move. The view you get is similar to one where you stand in a single spot and turn around in a full circle looking out toward the horizon.

Did You Know? ※

Many digital cameras come with a variety of software applications including digital photo-stitching applications. Check any CD-ROMs and written documentation that came with your camera to see if you have one.

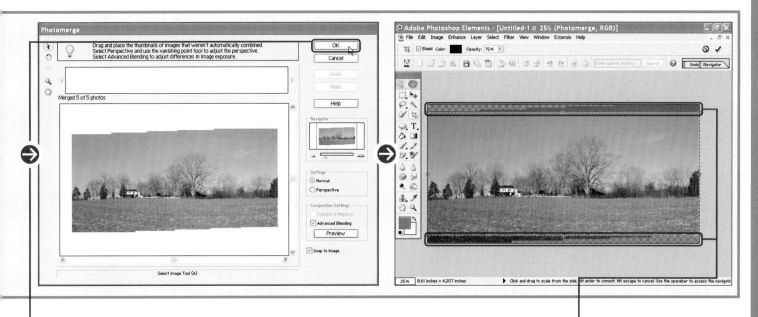

⑬ Click OK.

○ Photomerge begins the merge process.

○ The merged image opens in a new document window.

⑭ Select the Crop tool to crop the image.

HAND-COLOR
black-and-white photos

One fun and easy traditional photo technique you can do digitally is to simulate a hand-colored black-and-white photo. The traditional approach requires that you paint on a photographic print with special photographic paints that take time to dry and are easily smeared. Plus, you have brushes and mixing palettes to clean up. Painting digitally is easy and fun and the results can look wonderful if you take your time to select the right colors and paint carefully. Using a pen tablet like those made by Wacom makes this technique much more successful than if you use a mouse to paint.

The most effective way to create a hand-colored black-and-white photo effect is to create one layer for each color you use. Not only does this allow you to independently adjust each color with the Layer Opacity setting, but it also allows you to easily correct any mistakes. Additionally, you can apply Hue/Saturation changes to each color to get the perfect colors. If you want to build up each color gradually, you can vary the Opacity setting of the Brush tool.

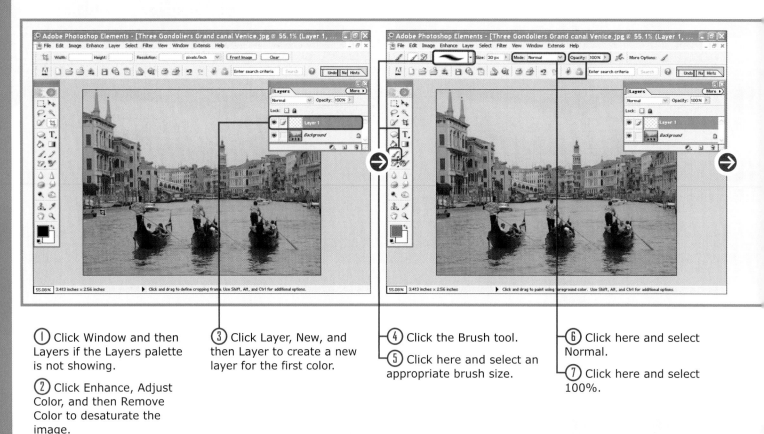

① Click Window and then Layers if the Layers palette is not showing.

② Click Enhance, Adjust Color, and then Remove Color to desaturate the image.

③ Click Layer, New, and then Layer to create a new layer for the first color.

④ Click the Brush tool.

⑤ Click here and select an appropriate brush size.

⑥ Click here and select Normal.

⑦ Click here and select 100%.

Did You Know? ☀

An easy way to make a
wonderful hand-colored black-
and-white photo is to open a color
photo and make a second copy. Convert
one copy to a black-and-white photo and
use the second copy as a color reference guide.
You can use the Eyedropper tool to pick a color to
use as the paint color for the black-and-white image.
Remember to make one layer for each different color
so that everything is reversible and changeable!

Did You Know? ☀

Most beginners who try the hand-colored black-and-white
photo technique use colors that are way too saturated
and bold. Traditional hand-colored black-and-white
photos are painted with subtle colors and usually only
a few colors are used.

DIFFICULTY LEVEL

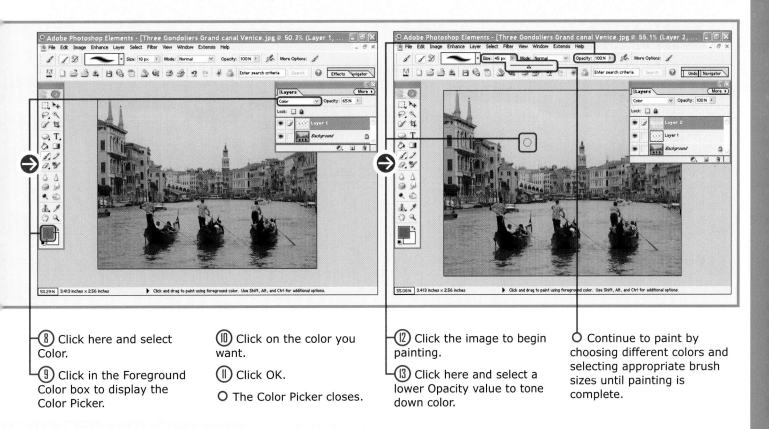

⑧ Click here and select
Color.

⑨ Click in the Foreground
Color box to display the
Color Picker.

⑩ Click on the color you
want.

⑪ Click OK.

○ The Color Picker closes.

⑫ Click the image to begin
painting.

⑬ Click here and select a
lower Opacity value to tone
down color.

○ Continue to paint by
choosing different colors and
selecting appropriate brush
sizes until painting is
complete.

PROTECT AND PRESERVE
original photo files

Saving a digital photo file is not all that hard. The hard part, if there is one, is learning when to save it. One of the most common mistakes made by those new to digital photography is to save a digital photo file over the original file after they have made edits to it with an image editor. When you do this, you no longer have an original image file, which can later prove to be a horrible loss. Even though you think you have made the photo look better, over time your skills and knowledge of digital photo editing will improve, and you will wish you had the original file.

Never overwrite your original image files; they have the most "picture information" you will ever have. Most editing sessions deteriorate the image even if they do look better, so you should protect your original digital photo files.

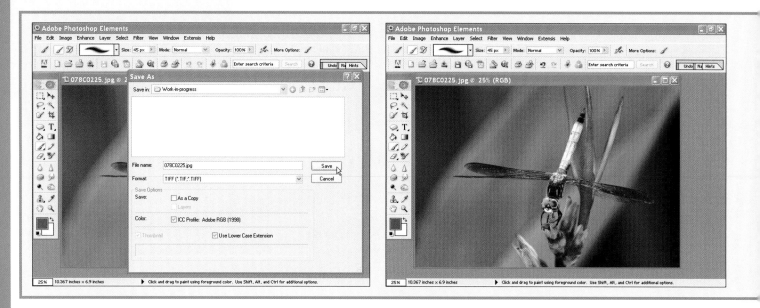

RENAME YOUR PROJECT

O After opening an original digital photo, you should save it to another folder, or save it under a different name or different file type to avoid overwriting the original file.

SAVE PROJECTS OFTEN

O Anytime you have spent more than 20 minutes or so editing a file, save the file under a different name or different file type to avoid overwriting the original file and to protect your work.

Caution! ☀

A common mistake is to make edits to an image and then increase the image size and sharpen it, before the image is saved. Anytime an image is increased in size, there will be some degradation in image quality. If you do not save your image after your edits are complete and before you have increased the image size, you will be saving a less-than-perfect image without any chance of going back.

69

DIFFICULTY LEVEL

Did You Know? ☀

You can make a digital photo appear to be more sharp using Adobe Photoshop Elements' Unsharp Mask command. This filter should only be applied to an image when there is no possibility that you will change the image size. The optimal settings for the Unsharp Mask are highly resolution dependent.

RETAIN ADJUSTMENT LAYERS

O Anytime you use adjustment layers to add additional elements to your image, you should save the file as a PSD file so that you can access your layers later.

O If you save it to a file format such as JPEG, you will never be able to access the separate layers again.

BEFORE SHARPENING AND RESIZING

O After you have completed all of your edits and before you have increased the size of the image or sharpened it, you should save the file.

O Sharpen an image and change its size only to output the image to a specific printer and display size.

RESIZE A BATCH
of digital photos

When you want to convert a batch of digital photo files to the same file format, or to the same size and resolution, you can easily do so with Adobe Photoshop Elements' Batch Processing command. You simply need to put all the digital photo files you want to convert, resize, and rename in one folder or a folder and subfolders. Then, specify how you want to convert them and which folder to use for the output folder.

You can also use Adobe Photoshop Elements' Batch Processing command to automatically rename a folder, or a folder and subfolders of image files, without making any changes to the files other than name changes. Just be sure to set the Convert File Type box to the type of files you want to rename, and uncheck the Convert Image Size box.

This is a useful feature for rapidly and easily converting an entire folder of digital photos to use in a slide show application or on a Web page, or for writing to a CD-ROM to have prints made at a digital photo-printing service company.

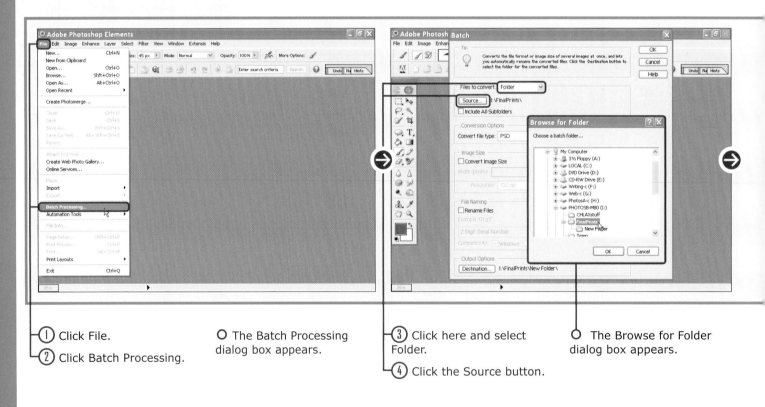

① Click File.

② Click Batch Processing.

○ The Batch Processing dialog box appears.

③ Click here and select Folder.

④ Click the Source button.

○ The Browse for Folder dialog box appears.

Did You Know? ※

When you have a folder of images that you want to convert and resize so that the longest side is equal to a specified length, Adobe Photoshop Elements' Batch Processing command cannot be used when some of the images are taller than they are wide while others are wider than they are tall. To work around this problem, create two folders and put all the images that are vertical in one folder and the horizontal photos in another folder. Then, run the Batch command on each folder.

#70

DIFFICULTY LEVEL

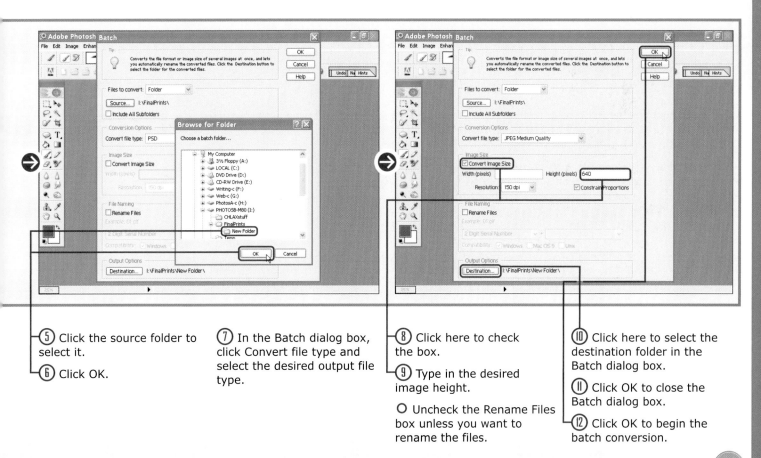

⑤ Click the source folder to select it.

⑥ Click OK.

⑦ In the Batch dialog box, click Convert file type and select the desired output file type.

⑧ Click here to check the box.

⑨ Type in the desired image height.

○ Uncheck the Rename Files box unless you want to rename the files.

⑩ Click here to select the destination folder in the Batch dialog box.

⑪ Click OK to close the Batch dialog box.

⑫ Click OK to begin the batch conversion.

Save photos for use on the
WEB

You can use Adobe Photoshop Element's Save As command to convert your digital photos into images that are perfectly suited to use on a Web page or to be e-mailed as an attachment. Although it is possible to resize your digital photo with the Image Size command and then save the resulting file using the Save As command, the Save for Web command has many advantages.

Anytime you save digital photos for use on a Web page, you are faced with a trade-off between image file size and image quality. The more you compress

the image, the faster it downloads and displays, yet the more an image is compressed, the more the image quality is reduced. The Save For Web dialog box allows you to view the original along with the compressed image side-by-side for comparison. This allows you to select the file type and the level of compression to optimize the tradeoff between file size and image quality. You can also change the image size and see the resulting file sizes displayed.

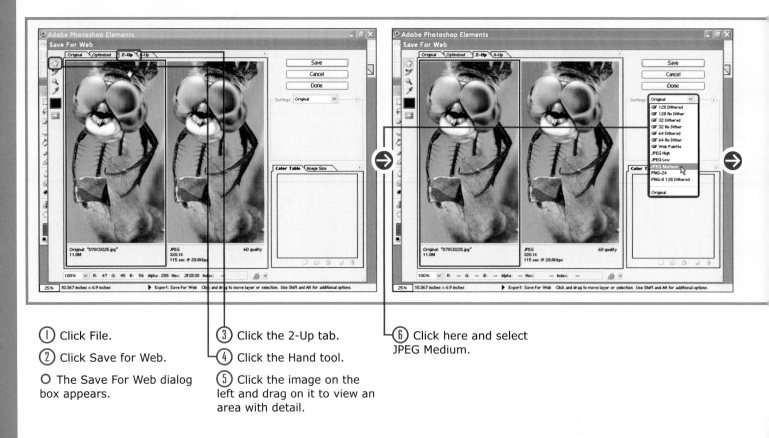

① Click File.

② Click Save for Web.

○ The Save For Web dialog box appears.

③ Click the 2-Up tab.

④ Click the Hand tool.

⑤ Click the image on the left and drag on it to view an area with detail.

⑥ Click here and select JPEG Medium.

Did You Know? ※

Adobe Photoshop Elements'
Save For Web dialog box offers
2-Up and 4-Up tabs that make it
easy for you to compare more than
one compression level and file format
side-by-side so that you can select the
right amount of compression while minimizing
image degradation. This is a useful feature
because few visitors will take time to view all of
the photos in an online gallery if they take too long
to download or suffer from too much image degradation
due to excessive compression.

Did You Know? ※

You can fine-tune compression levels with the
Quality slider found in Adobe Photoshop Elements'
Save For Web dialog box.

#71

DIFFICULTY LEVEL

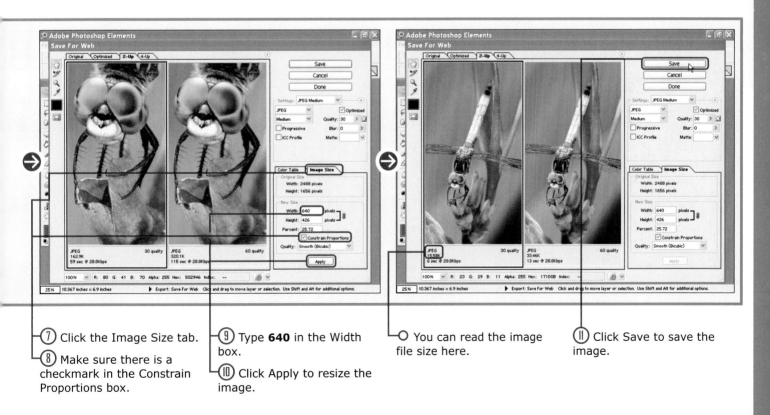

⑦ Click the Image Size tab.

⑧ Make sure there is a checkmark in the Constrain Proportions box.

⑨ Type **640** in the Width box.

⑩ Click Apply to resize the image.

─○ You can read the image file size here.

⑪ Click Save to save the image.

Adjust Tonal Range and Color with Adobe Photoshop Elements

The vast majority of problems from which digital photographs suffer fall in the category of tonal range and color. Such issues include not having enough contrast, having too much backlighting, or too little foreground lighting, improper color casts, dull colors, or colors that are too bright. Whether the problems result from bad lighting situations, incorrect camera settings, or just a bad scanner device, you can always find ways to correct your images with a little help from Photoshop Elements.

Photoshop Elements offers a variety of features that you can utilize to adjust your digital images. By far the most popular tool for making corrections is the Levels dialog

box, which you can use to fix both contrast and color problems. You can also apply a variety of specific filters to lighten, darken, and blend layers in an image.

When deciding how to fix a tonal range or color problem, start by copying the background layer. Adding layers allows you to experiment with various features and editing techniques without accidentally damaging or making permanent changes to the original image layer. Use specialized adjustment layers to focus your edits on specific types of problems, such as Hue/Saturation or Brightness/Contrast. Adjustment layers give you direct access to related tools for making corrections.

TOP 100

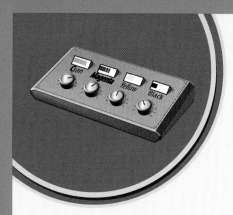

CHECK PHOTO EXPOSURE
with the histogram

You should first examine a photo carefully and determine an overall editing strategy before you begin making edits. One of the first things you should check is the tonal range, which you can adjust using the Levels dialog box.

The Levels dialog box gives you a good graphical representation, called a *histogram*, of how well or how poorly your image was exposed. The histogram plots out the light and dark pixels in an image in terms of intensity. It also shows you how much contrast the image has, displaying

how many pixels are in each of 256 tonal ranges. The more intense the grouping of pixels in an image, the taller the histogram reading for that particular tonal area of the image. For example, a histogram showing a large count of dark pixels may need adjustments in tone or contrast to correct the image.

As you examine the histogram shown in the Levels dialog box, be aware that there is no such thing as a perfect histogram.

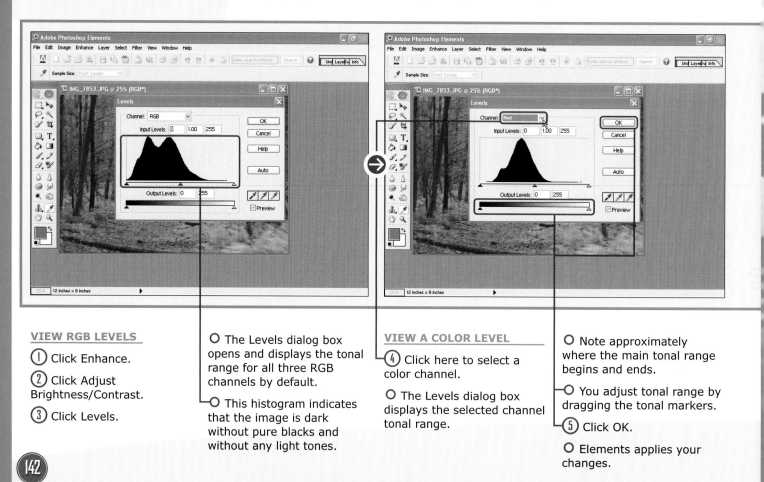

VIEW RGB LEVELS

① Click Enhance.

② Click Adjust Brightness/Contrast.

③ Click Levels.

O The Levels dialog box opens and displays the tonal range for all three RGB channels by default.

O This histogram indicates that the image is dark without pure blacks and without any light tones.

VIEW A COLOR LEVEL

④ Click here to select a color channel.

O The Levels dialog box displays the selected channel tonal range.

O Note approximately where the main tonal range begins and ends.

O You adjust tonal range by dragging the tonal markers.

⑤ Click OK.

O Elements applies your changes.

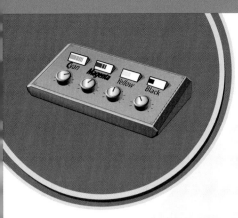

CHECK FOR COLOR CASTS
with the Info palette

73

DIFFICULTY LEVEL

Photoshop Elements includes a handy tool, called the Info palette, that you can use to evaluate the color values in a digital image. The Info palette allows you to check different pixels in an image to compare Red, Green, and Blue channel values. One of the best uses of this tool is to compare the color casts of two photos, such as an edited photo and original photo. For example, you might check how your edits affect skin tone color from one photo to the other, or you might

check how much of a color boost occurs in a particular area of the photo after applying a filter.

As you move the mouse pointer over an image, the Info palette displays the numeric values for colors that appear beneath the pointer at any given spot on the photo. By default, the Info palette uses RGB mode to read a photo. You can also view Grayscale, Web, and HSB color values.

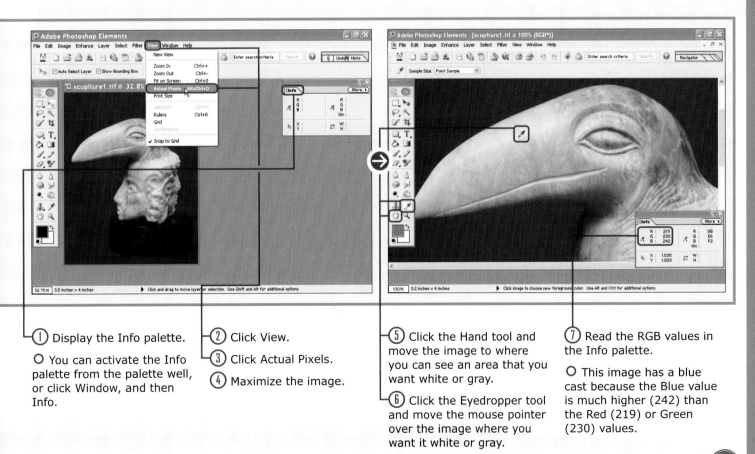

① Display the Info palette.

○ You can activate the Info palette from the palette well, or click Window, and then Info.

② Click View.

③ Click Actual Pixels.

④ Maximize the image.

⑤ Click the Hand tool and move the image to where you can see an area that you want white or gray.

⑥ Click the Eyedropper tool and move the mouse pointer over the image where you want it white or gray.

⑦ Read the RGB values in the Info palette.

○ This image has a blue cast because the Blue value is much higher (242) than the Red (219) or Green (230) values.

Fix
UNDER- OR OVEREXPOSED
photos

One of the most common problems with photos is that they are either underexposed or overexposed. While this is often a subjective determination, you can quickly lighten or darken an image by tinkering with a few of the layer blending modes available in Photoshop Elements. Blending modes allow you to change the way pixels mix between two layers of an image. For example, the Screen blending mode, when applied to an underexposed photo, always makes the image colors appear lighter. The Screen blending mode examines each channel's color and

multiplies the inverse of the blend layer and the base layer.

The Multiply blending mode makes the image colors darken, which is ideal for overexposed photos. The Multiply blending mode examines each channel's color values and multiplies the base color by the blend layer color. You also use the Multiply blending mode to intensify image colors.

With either blending mode, you can fine-tune the exposure lighting by adjusting the layer's Opacity setting.

ADJUST UNDEREXPOSURE

○ This photo of a seaside building appears a bit underexposed.

① Create a copy of the background layer in the Layers palette.

Note: You can create a quick layer copy by selecting Layer, Duplicate Layer, and clicking OK.

② Click here to select Screen mode.

○ Elements immediately lightens the image.

○ To make the blending effect more subtle, click and drag the Opacity slider to adjust exposure brightness.

○ Elements reduces the underexposure by lightening the image.

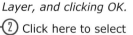

Did You Know? ⁂

Although you may be tempted to apply the Brightness and Contrast feature in Elements to correct exposure and contrast problems, this feature does not correct overly light or dark images. Instead, it either raises the brightness values in an image to make all the pixels brighter, or lowers the values to make all the pixels darker. For most photos, you do not need to adjust all the pixels, just the ones affected by the exposure problem. For best results, use the blending modes and adjustment layers to correct exposure problems.

#74

DIFFICULTY LEVEL

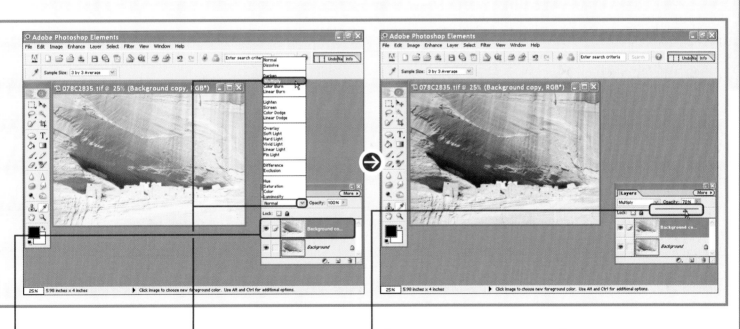

ADJUST OVEREXPOSURE

○ This photo of ancient Indian dwellings appears a bit overexposed.

① Create a copy of the background layer.

Note: You can create a quick layer copy by selecting Layer, Duplicate Layer, and clicking OK.

② Click here to select Multiply mode.

○ Elements immediately darkens the image.

○ To make the blending effect more subtle, you can click and drag the Opacity slider to adjust the exposure brightness.

○ Elements reduces the overexposure by darkening the dwellings.

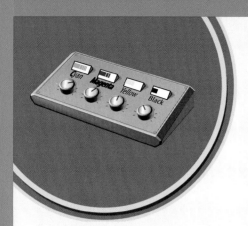

Understanding
CONTRAST

A good technique for improving any digital photograph is to look for ways to enhance the contrast in an image. By definition, *contrast* is the difference between the darkest and lightest areas in a photo; the greater the difference, the higher the contrast. Photos with low contrast typically appear a bit muddy or fuzzy, without any clear distinctions between details in the images.

Contrast in black and white photos works a bit differently than contrast in color photos. Grayscale images display contrast in terms of brightness levels,

or luminosity. Color images also have luminosity, but it shows up in color hue and saturation.

It is often amazing how a few tweaks of an image's hue and saturation levels can enhance contrast. Photoshop Elements includes several useful tools for adjusting image contrast, one of the best being the Levels dialog box. To summon the Levels dialog box, click Enhance, Adjust Brightness/Contrast, and then Levels from the menu bar. By making a few adjustments to the shadows, midtones, and highlights in a photo, you can quickly achieve contrast that was previously lacking.

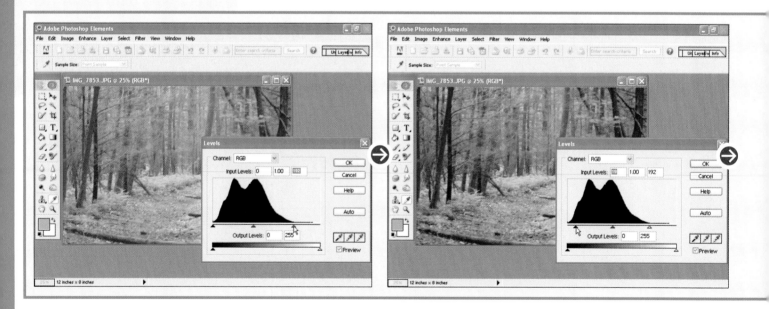

O In this photo, the lack of contrast results in a general fuzziness to the appearance of the trees.

O In this example, the contrast is enhanced slightly by intensifying the highlights.

Did You Know? ☀

Learning to read the histogram, the graphical diagram in the Levels dialog box, is a great way to understand contrast issues existing in your photos. The histogram displays the tonal range of values in your image and shows you exactly where shadows, midtones, and highlights are at the strongest or weakest in the image. See task #72 for more information.

#75

DIFFICULTY LEVEL

Did You Know? ☀

Sharpening filters can also help to improve the contrast in your photos. The most popular filter for sharpening images in Elements is the Unsharp Mask. Using this filter takes a bit of experimentation using the three available controls. To apply the filter, choose Filter, Sharpen, and then Unsharp Mask. This opens the Unsharp Mask dialog box where you can make and preview your adjustments.

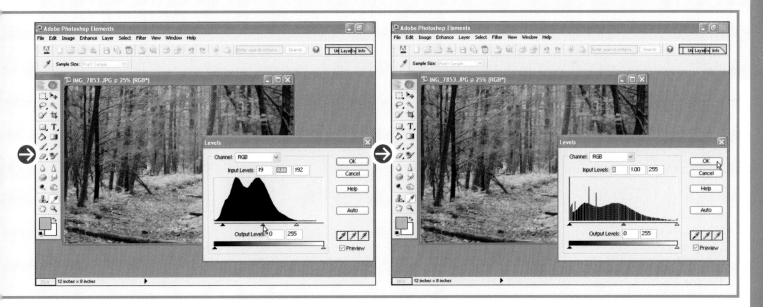

O Next, the shadows are intensified to create clearer contrast between light and dark areas.

O The most useful tool for improving contrast is the Levels dialog box, where you can adjust shadows, midtones, and highlights to enhance image contrast.

O Note the levels of intensities throughout the tonal range.

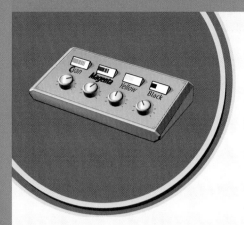

RESTORE IMAGE DETAIL
by setting black and white points

You can use the Levels dialog box to specify black and white points within a photo. Targeting the darkest and brightest pixels in an image can help you restore image detail, tonal range, and contrast. After specifying new black and white points in an image, the full tonal range stretches out between the two settings to increase contrast. The result is often a dramatically improved image.

For example, when you target a white area in a photo, Photoshop Elements remaps and redefines the tonal information throughout the image,

changing a dingy image into one with clearer white and black areas. All the other pixel values in the image also adjust in proportion to the new highlight values.

Elements' eyedropper tools help you target colors for highlights, shadows, and neutral grays. Because the tools target color changes, they work best for color correction problems rather than exposure problems. The key to setting black and white points is first identifying representative shadows and highlights in your image.

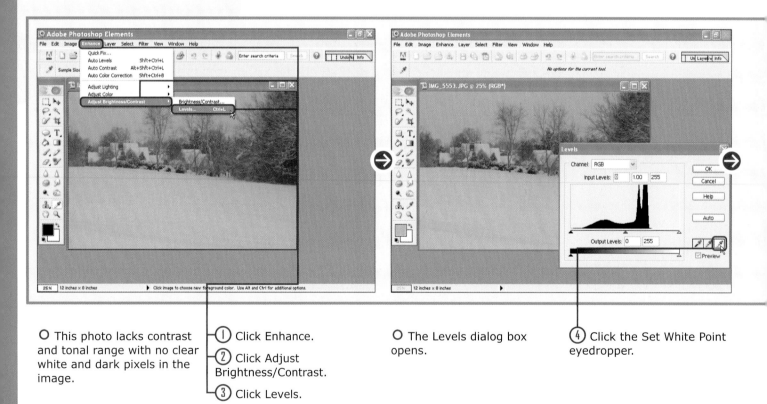

○ This photo lacks contrast and tonal range with no clear white and dark pixels in the image.

① Click Enhance.

② Click Adjust Brightness/Contrast.

③ Click Levels.

○ The Levels dialog box opens.

④ Click the Set White Point eyedropper.

Caulion! ☼

Be careful where you click the Levels eyedropper tools. If you click the Set White Point eyedropper on an area that is not representative of white in your photo, for example, other lighter tones in the image are affected and may become overly whitened. This may result in a loss of detail in your image and an excessively contrasty image. The same problem can occur if you click on an area that is not truly black. Picking the wrong points when setting the black and white points can result in strange and inaccurate colors.

DIFFICULTY LEVEL

Did You Know? ☼

You can reset the Levels values back to their original values by pressing Alt, which turns the Cancel button into a Reset button; then, click on the Reset button and you are ready to try new settings or click Cancel to close the Levels dialog box.

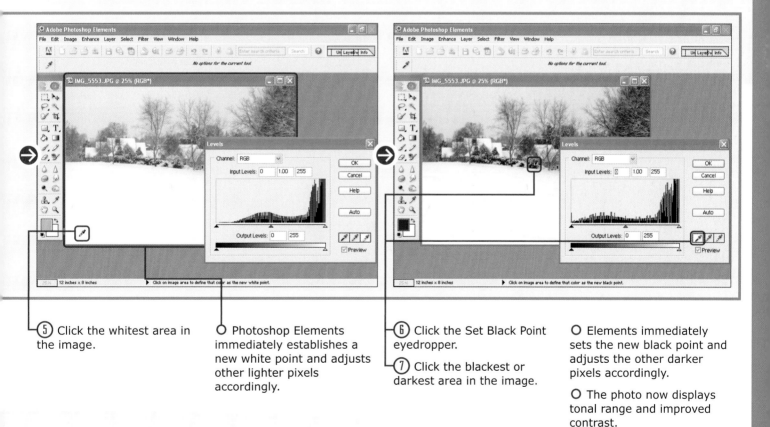

⑤ Click the whitest area in the image.

◯ Photoshop Elements immediately establishes a new white point and adjusts other lighter pixels accordingly.

⑥ Click the Set Black Point eyedropper.

⑦ Click the blackest or darkest area in the image.

◯ Elements immediately sets the new black point and adjusts the other darker pixels accordingly.

◯ The photo now displays tonal range and improved contrast.

Improve image contrast with a
LEVELS LAYER

You can create a Levels adjustment layer to improve the contrast in an image. You can use adjustment layers in Photoshop Elements to make changes to a photo without altering the underlying original image. With adjustment layers, you can apply all kinds of changes to colors, tonal range, and contrast to a copy of the original image layer. The original image remains intact. After you are happy with your adjustments, you can flatten the image and apply the changes to the actual image layer. If you do not like the changes, you can simply discard the Levels

adjustment layer. To learn more about creating adjustment layers, see task #66.

A Levels adjustment layer is directly connected to the Levels dialog box. As such, you can easily summon the Levels dialog box at any time to make changes to the shadows, midtones, and highlights of an image. The Input sliders in the dialog box allow you to remap black and white points in your image to make improvements to the image's overall contrast.

○ This photo appears a bit dull and lacking in contrast.

① Display the Layers palette.

Note: You can activate the Layers palette from the palette well, or click Window, Layers.

② Click here to select Levels.

○ Elements adds a new adjustment layer to the Layers palette and the Levels dialog box opens.

③ Drag the Input Levels highlight slider to just inside of where the lightest image information begins.

○ The pixels in the highlights immediately lighten.

Did You Know? ※

To keep your edits organized, consider naming any new adjustment layers you add to the Layers palette. For example, if you use a Levels adjustment layer to correct contrast problems, name the layer Contrast to remind you of the purpose of the layer. To name a layer, double-click the default layer name in the Layers palette and type a new name. Press Enter and Photoshop Elements saves the new name.

#77

DIFFICULTY LEVEL

Did You Know? ※

You can apply an adjustment layer to part of your image instead of the entire image. To do so, make a selection with a selection tool before creating the adjustment layer. Doing this also gives you continued control over the selection, as you can also adjust it with the Opacity slider or change the Blend mode.

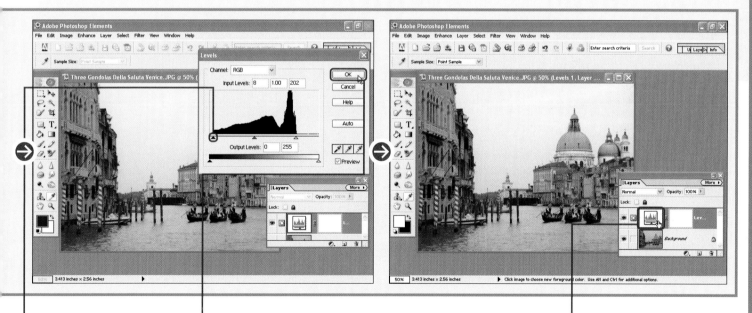

④ Drag the Input Levels shadow slider to just inside of where the darkest image information begins.

○ The pixels in the shadows immediately darken.

⑤ Click OK.

○ Elements applies the changes to the adjustment layer and the photo's contrast improves.

○ To return to the Levels dialog box at any time for more adjustments, simply double-click the Levels thumbnail.

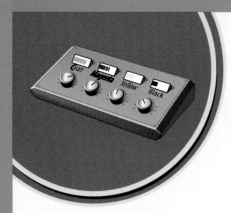

ADJUST BACKLIGHTING
with the Adjust Backlighting command

If your photo suffers from an overexposed background, such as a sky that is brighter than the subject matter, you can make corrections using the Adjust Backlighting command. This command allows you to reduce the brightness from the sun or other reflective light sources and to bring out background details. For example, reducing the brightness of the sky in some photos can reveal details in clouds.

The Adjust Backlighting filter works by darkening overexposed areas in an image. Tonal variations for this filter are measured in

values that range from 0 to 100. The larger the value setting number, the darker the image's background appears.

If you prefer to keep the foreground or subject matter unaffected by the filter, select it and copy it to another layer in the Layers palette before applying this technique to the layer containing the overexposed background.

To precisely fix exposure problems, you can use the Levels dialog box to fine-tune the shadows, midtones, and highlights.

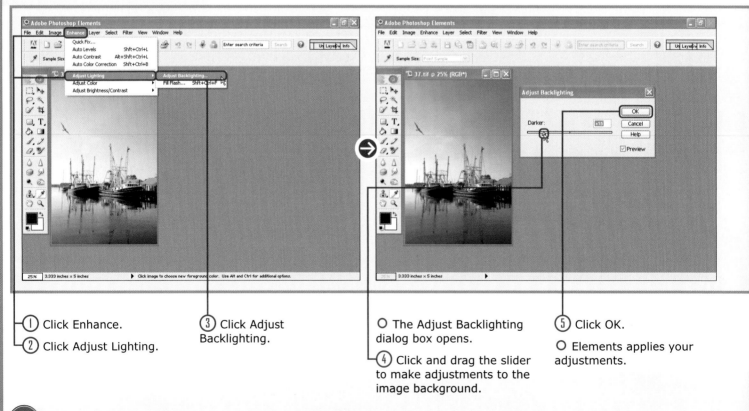

① Click Enhance.

② Click Adjust Lighting.

③ Click Adjust Backlighting.

○ The Adjust Backlighting dialog box opens.

④ Click and drag the slider to make adjustments to the image background.

⑤ Click OK.

○ Elements applies your adjustments.

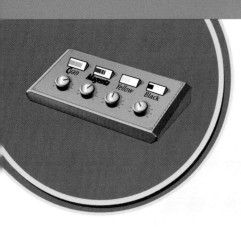

REVEAL DETAIL IN SHADOWS
with the Fill Flash filter

#79

DIFFICULTY LEVEL

You can use the Fill Flash filter in Photoshop Elements to lighten the shadows in a photo. Pictures that you take in bright light often produce very dark shadows in the foreground objects, resulting in very little detail. For example, if you take a picture of someone against a bright background, the person's face often turns into a silhouette with shadows obscuring the details of their face. By applying a Fill Flash filter, you can bring out the shadow details and enhance the overall image appearance.

The Fill Flash filter creates the illusion of an actual fill flash that professional photographers use to fill in light for darker lighting conditions. You can use this filter to adjust photos that suffer from poor foreground lighting.

The Fill Flash filter offers two controls for adjusting the fill flash effect. You can use the Lighter control to lighten the shadows. You can use the Saturation control to lower the saturation if the lightening adjustment creates an oversaturated image.

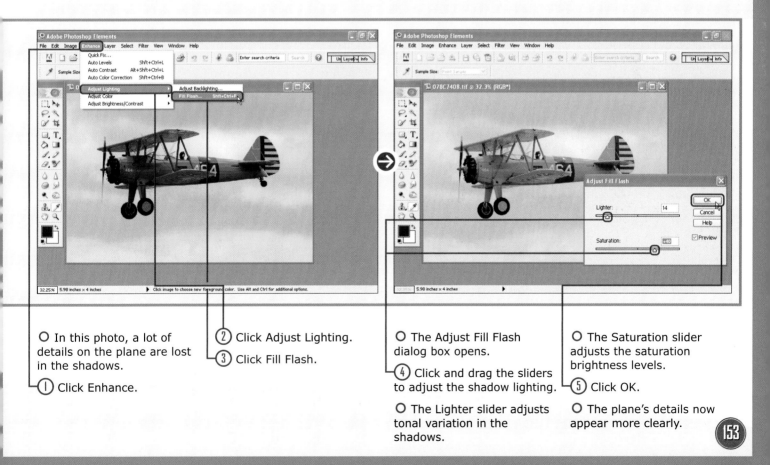

O In this photo, a lot of details on the plane are lost in the shadows.

(1) Click Enhance.

(2) Click Adjust Lighting.

(3) Click Fill Flash.

O The Adjust Fill Flash dialog box opens.

(4) Click and drag the sliders to adjust the shadow lighting.

O The Lighter slider adjusts tonal variation in the shadows.

O The Saturation slider adjusts the saturation brightness levels.

(5) Click OK.

O The plane's details now appear more clearly.

153

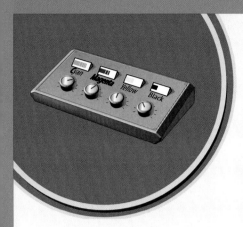

LIGHTEN OR DARKEN
a selected portion of a photo

In some cases, only certain areas of your photo may need lightening or darkening to improve the photo's appearance. Perhaps only a portion of someone's face needs lightening, or a specific highlight needs toning down. You can select an area of your photo to edit in Photoshop Elements and then make adjustments to the shadows, midtones, and highlights in the image using the Levels dialog box. The remaining portions of the image are not affected by any changes you apply.

Depending on the level of detail in your photo, you may find selecting a specific portion of the image for edits time-consuming. Photoshop Elements offers a variety of selection tools to assist you. To learn more about using the selection tools in the Toolbox, see task #64.

For best results, make a copy of the background or other layer you want to edit, and then make your changes to the layer copy. This leaves the original photo layer intact in case you do not like the results of your changes.

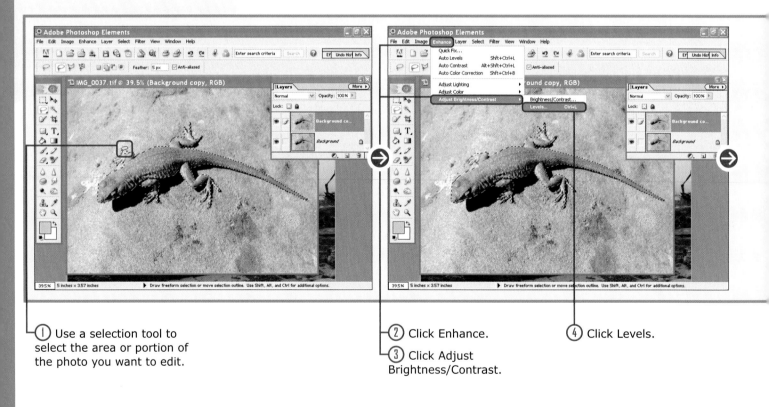

① Use a selection tool to select the area or portion of the photo you want to edit.

② Click Enhance.

③ Click Adjust Brightness/Contrast.

④ Click Levels.

Did You Know? ※

You can quickly create an inverse of a selected area in a photo to select the remaining portion of the image. To do so, click Select, and then Inverse.

Did You Know? ※

You can save yourself some time and effort by saving your selections. For example, if you painstakingly trace a detailed subject in a photo, such as the lizard shown in the steps below, you can save the selection to reuse again with other edits. To save a selection, click Select, and then Save Selection. The Save Selection dialog box opens. In this dialog box, type a name for the selection and click OK. To reuse the selection again, click Select, Load Selection, and specify which selection to apply.

DIFFICULTY LEVEL

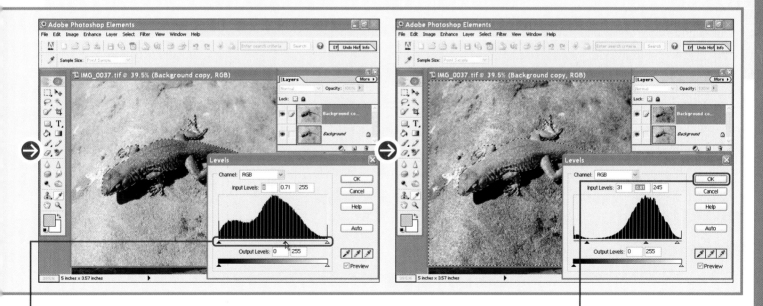

○ The Levels dialog box opens.

⑤ Click and drag the shadows, midtones, or highlights sliders to lighten or darken the selected portion of the photo.

○ This example shows that the lizard's midtones are darkened while the background remains the same.

○ In this example, the reverse of the image is selected and darkened while the lizard remains the same.

⑥ Click OK.

○ Elements applies your changes to the photo.

REMOVE COLOR CASTS
with the Color Cast command

One of the most common color problems from which photos can suffer is unwanted color casts. This problem frequently occurs when shooting indoor scenes using daylight film with improper ambient lighting. The result is often a photo with a greenish tint. You can also introduce color cast problems by improperly setting the white balance on a digital camera, or using poorly scanned photos. Photoshop Elements includes several tools for eliminating color cast problems. This task focuses on using the Color Cast command to correct unwanted color casts.

The key to using the Color Cast feature is to apply it around the photo paying particular attention to areas of the image that should be gray, white, or black. Doing so causes Elements to change the overall mixture of colors in the image to compensate for the improper color cast. Applying the tool to areas that are already true gray, white, or black does not produce the best results. Elements checks the sampled area to which you applied it and adds equal amounts of red, green, and blue. Elements also shifts the remaining colors to create a neutral state.

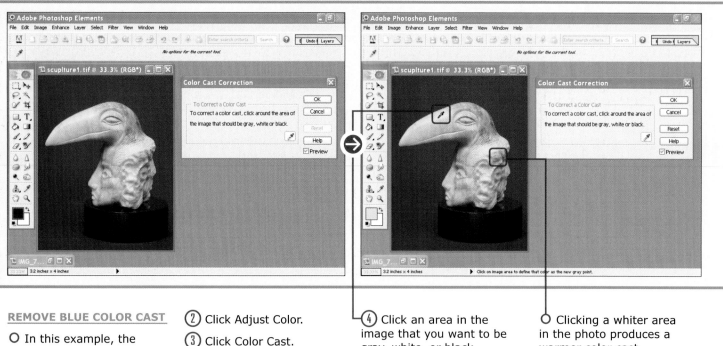

REMOVE BLUE COLOR CAST

O In this example, the photo has a bluish color cast.

① Click Enhance.

② Click Adjust Color.

③ Click Color Cast.

O The Color Cast Correction dialog box opens.

④ Click an area in the image that you want to be gray, white, or black.

O Clicking a whiter area in the photo produces a warmer color cast.

Did You Know? ※

You can also use the Color Variations feature to correct simple color cast problems. The Color Variations feature allows you to adjust color balance, contrast, and saturation. To use this feature, click Enhance, Adjust Color, and then Color Variations. This opens the Color Variation dialog box. Next, click a tonal range to apply adjustments to different tones in your image. To add a color or subtract a color, click one of the thumbnails. The After preview area shows the results. You can continue clicking the thumbnail to increase or decrease the adjustment.

DIFFICULTY LEVEL

REMOVE GREEN COLOR CAST

O In this photo, the green colors in the leaves and ferns give the image a greenish cast.

① Clicking a darker area among the tree trunks produces a grayer color cast.

② Click OK.

O Elements applies the changes to the photo.

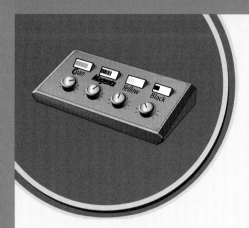

ADJUST COLOR
with a Hue/Saturation layer

You can create a Hue/Saturation adjustment layer to make adjustments to the colors in a photo. You use the Hue/Saturation filter controls to change the hue of a photo, to increase or decrease color saturation throughout the image, or to adjust the lightness values of the colors. A Hue/Saturation adjustment layer is directly connected to the Hue/Saturation dialog box.

The hue level control allows you to change colors based on Elements' color wheel and set different color hues. Moving the control's slider represents a

move around the color wheel. The saturation control allows you to adjust the purity or intensity of the colors. The lightness control lets you set a brightness level for the colors.

You can choose to edit all the colors at once, or you can edit preset color ranges, such as the yellow or green colors in a photo. The Master setting encompasses all the colors in a photo and appears by default in the Hue/Saturation dialog box. To edit a color range instead, you must first specify the range before adjusting the slider controls.

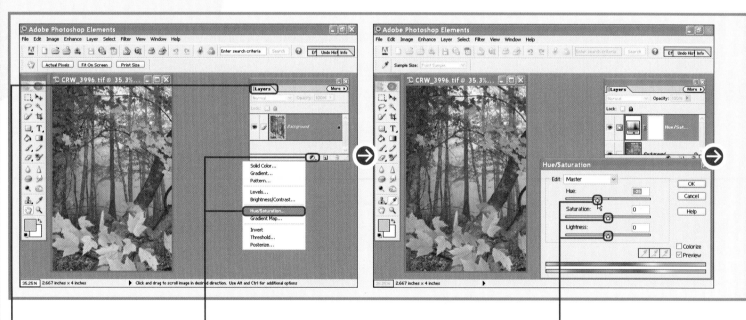

① Display the Layers palette.

Note: You can activate the Layers palette from the palette well, or click Window, Layers.

② Click the Create new fill or adjustment layer button and choose Hue/Saturation.

Note: See task #66 to learn more about adjustment layers.

○ Elements adds a new adjustment layer to the Layers palette and the Hue/Saturation dialog box opens.

③ Click and drag a slider to adjust the color hue, saturation, or lightness.

○ In this example, the hue slider changes the color of the image, particularly the leaves.

DIFFICULTY LEVEL

Did You Know? ⁂

You can use the Levels dialog box to intensify selected color channels in an image. For example, if you want to boost the colors in the Red channel only, you can specify the channel first and then adjust the shadows, midtones, and highlights sliders. See task 77 to learn how to create a Levels adjustment layer.

Did You Know? ⁂

You can also use the Multiply blending mode to strengthen colors in a photo. Duplicate the layer you want to adjust, and then apply the Multiply blending mode by clicking the blending mode button in the Layers palette and selecting Multiply. You can then adjust the color intensity of the effect with the Opacity control.

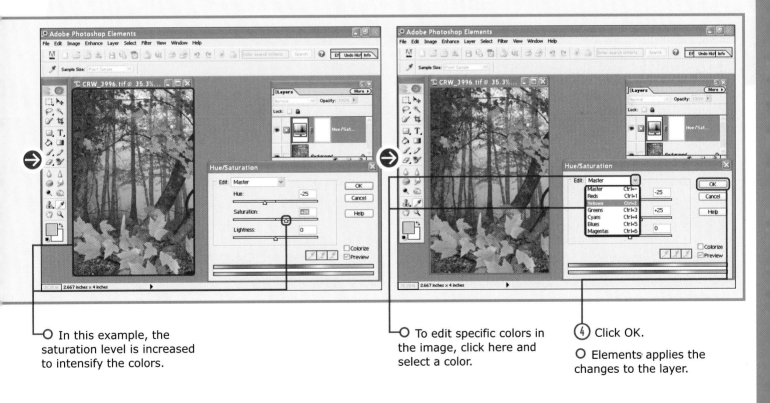

─O In this example, the saturation level is increased to intensify the colors.

─O To edit specific colors in the image, click here and select a color.

④ Click OK.

O Elements applies the changes to the layer.

CHAPTER 9

Make Photographic Prints

Even though taking pictures with a digital camera makes it easy to share digital photos electronically — on a Web page, as an e-mail attachment, or on a computer or TV screen — a photographic print on paper is still what photography is all about to many people. You can make photo-quality prints from digital photo files in many ways, including printing them on a desktop photo printer, ordering prints from an online photo-printing service, or using a local photo-processing lab.

Before you are ready to make prints, however, you may need to perform some basic image editing to get the best results. To make prints that look like the images on your computer screen, you need to take the time to

calibrate your monitor and create or select the correct color profiles for the printer, ink, and media you are using.

Besides performing basic photo corrections to your digital photos, you also need to make sure that the aspect ratio is correct for the print size you want, that the image size is large enough for the print size you want, and that it has been sharpened for the target printer. If you are using your own desktop photo printer, you may also want to use Adobe Photoshop Elements or another similar image editor to precisely position a photo on a page, create multiple photo page layouts, and print thumbnail sheets to use as indexes.

TOP 100

Understanding
COLOR
MANAGEMENT

Your digital camera, computer screen, and printer all reproduce color differently, and each one has different limitations on how they can display color. *Color management* is a system of hardware and software products that have been configured to ensure accurate color across all devices. In other words, if you have implemented color management properly on your hardware, the "barn red" barn in front of the soft pale blue sky you see on your computer monitor will show up as "barn red" against the same soft pale blue sky in your prints.

A few important steps for getting your hardware color managed are calibrating your computer display, choosing and using appropriate color profiles for each print device you use, and using the right color profiles for the specific combination of printer, ink, and paper you are using. Taking, editing, and printing digital photos can be a joy and easy to do when you have accurate color across both your hardware and your software. Without color management, the same process of taking, editing, and printing digital photos can become frustrating, causing you to waste money on paper and ink while creating unacceptable prints.

O The LCD screen on the Canon PowerShot G3 displays a thumbnail image of a photo of orchids.

O This computer monitor displays the orchids as they looked when the photo was taken.

#83

DIFFICULTY LEVEL

Did You Know?

You can calibrate your Windows PC monitor using Adobe Gamma, which is a software utility added to the Control Panel when you install Adobe Photoshop Elements. To access the Control Panel, click the Start button and select Control Panel from the menu. If you are using a Mac, you can use Apple's ColorSync utility, which can be found in the Systems Preferences. Be sure to adjust your monitor in the lighting conditions you normally work in.

Did You Know?

The most accurate way to calibrate your computer monitor or LCD is to use a monitor spider like the MonacoOPTIX Colorimeter for LCD and CRT displays (www.monacosys.com). This hardware product attaches to your computer display so that it can read colors displayed by the monitor and create an accurate color profile.

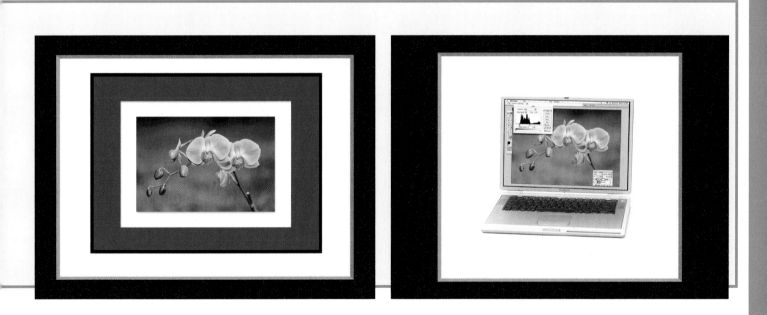

○ The orchids look the same on this print as they did on the monitor and as when the photo was taken.

○ The orchids on this Mac PowerBook G4 LCD looks the same as they did on the print, the PC monitor, and as they did when the photo was taken.

CROP A PHOTO
to a specified size

You can crop your photos when you want to keep only a certain part of the photo, or when you need to make a photo meet specific width and height requirements. Adobe Photoshop Elements offers two useful tools for cropping images. You can select the part of the image that you want to keep using the Rectangular Marquee tool and then select the Image, Crop menu command to crop the image. Alternatively, you can use the Crop tool, which has a few extra

features that are useful for cropping images precisely as you want them.

Using the Crop tool, not only can you crop to a fixed aspect ratio, but you can also crop to a fixed size specified in inches and at a specified printer resolution. Additionally, the Crop tool enables you to drag the edges of the selection to select exactly the area you want; it even enables you to rotate the image to end up with a vertical photo.

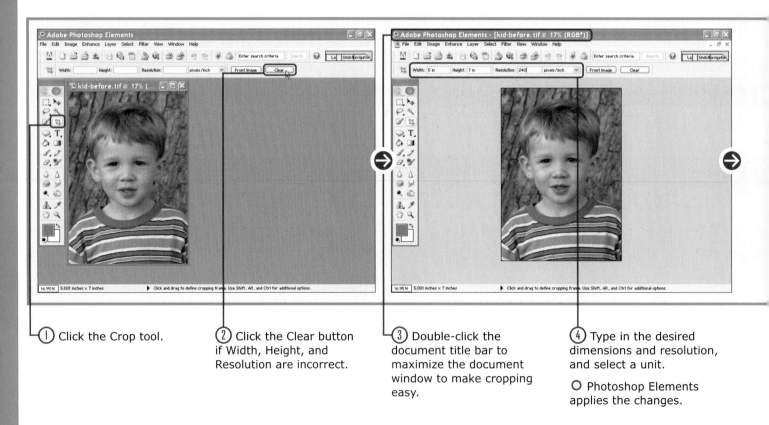

① Click the Crop tool.

② Click the Clear button if Width, Height, and Resolution are incorrect.

③ Double-click the document title bar to maximize the document window to make cropping easy.

④ Type in the desired dimensions and resolution, and select a unit.

○ Photoshop Elements applies the changes.

DIFFICULTY LEVEL

Did You Know?

You can increase or decrease the size of the selection by clicking on one of the corners of the selection marquee and dragging it. If you entered values in the Width and Height box, the Crop tool automatically maintains the aspect ratio.

You can move the entire selection marquee by clicking inside the marquee and dragging the cursor.

If you want to crop to the outside of the photo, click outside the photo and drag the selection marquee to where you want it to be.

Caution!

When you crop an image and type a value into the Resolution box, you *may* be enlarging your image so much that it will decrease the image quality.

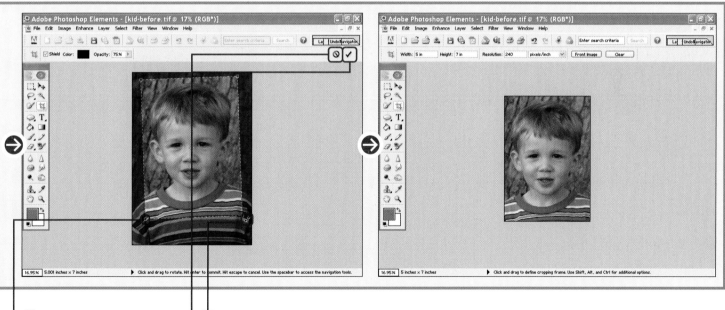

⑤ Click and drag a corner of the selection marquee to select the area of the photo you want.

⑥ Place the mouse pointer outside the selection marquee.

O The cursor changes to indicate that you can rotate the image.

⑦ Click and drag to rotate the selection until it appears as you like.

⑧ Click here to apply the crop.

O To cancel the crop, click here.

O This final image has been cropped, resized, and rotated to be vertical.

LARGE PRINT

The largest size print you can make with your digital camera is limited by the pixel size of your camera, the quality of the photo you want to enlarge, and your tolerance for image degradation due to image upsampling. A 4-megapixel camera has more pixels than a 3-megapixel camera and can therefore be used to make larger prints. Images with low digital noise and smooth tonal gradations are better candidates to use for large prints than images taken at high ISO settings with lots of digital noise — unless the intent is to get that effect.

To determine how large a print you can make with any given image, you need to experiment and examine the prints. To determine the optimal print size, you divide the pixel dimensions by the "optimal print DPI" for the printer or print service you intend to use. For example, most Epson printers make excellent prints at 240 DPI. Hence, a 3.8-megapixel camera that provides a 1,536 x 2,480 pixel image would make an *optimal* print size of 6.4" x 10.3" — enough for an excellent 5" x 7" print, but not enough for an 8" x 10" print.

① Click Image, Resize, and then Image Size.

О The Image Size dialog box appears.

② Type the target printer DPI in the Resolution box.

О Make sure a check mark is in the Constrain Proportions box to keep the aspect ratio constant.

③ Type the desired width or height in either the Pixel Dimensions area or the Document size area.

О Notice the change in image size.

О Optimal print size is 1,575 x 2,100 pixels at 240 DPI.

О This 6.06MB image is near optimal print size, and it shows no loss in image quality.

Did You Know?

Some printers do a better job of increasing image size, or *upsampling,* than can be done with Adobe Photoshop Elements' Image Size command. One such printer is the Lightjet 5000 printer, which has its own hardware-based interpolation. The Lightjet 5000 printer can make quality prints as large as 30" x 40" with images from a 3-megapixel camera. To get a quality print that you have increased in size to such a degree requires an exceptional digital photo and skill with an image editor.

Caution!

When enlarging any image, you should always save the upsampled image to a new file and not overwrite the original image. Writing over the original image leaves you with nothing but the lesser-quality image.

O This photo has been upsampled to be 1,920 x 2,560 pixels, which makes an 11" x 14" print at 240 DPI.

O A noticeable but acceptable amount of image degradation is visible in this 26.5MB image.

O This photo has been upsampled to be 3,840 x 5,120 pixels, which makes a 16" x 20" print at 240 DPI.

O Substantial and unacceptable image degradation, caused by over-increasing image size, appears in this 56.3MB image.

SHARPEN
a digital photo

Most photos taken with digital cameras look soft; that is, they do not look as sharply focused as they could. This is primarily due to the fact that digital cameras capture "digitally." Smaller megapixel cameras do not have sufficient resolution to produce the sharp-looking photos that you can obtain with a film camera that records in analog and can capture the important details found on the edges of elements in a photo.

However, using an image editor like Adobe Photoshop Elements, you can make an image look

as sharp as any photo taken with a film camera. One easy way to increase the *perceived* sharpness of a photo is to use the Unsharp Mask filter found in most image-editing applications.

You need to use different Unsharp Mask settings for the same photo when using it in different sizes for different purposes. For example, the best settings for an 800 x 640-pixel image that you want to use on a Web page are entirely different than the settings you need to make a high-resolution print.

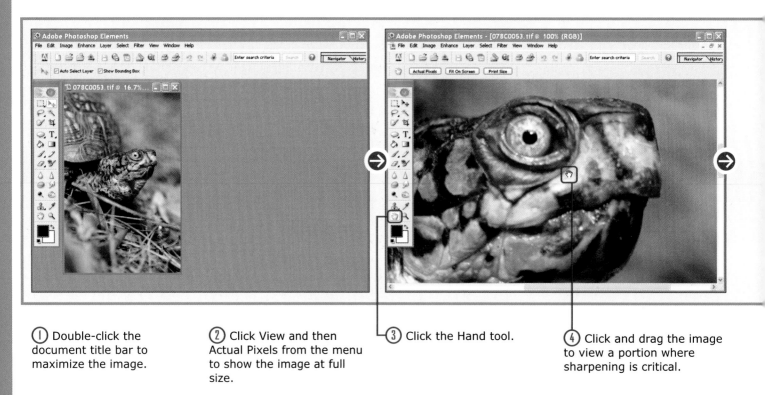

① Double-click the document title bar to maximize the image.

② Click View and then Actual Pixels from the menu to show the image at full size.

③ Click the Hand tool.

④ Click and drag the image to view a portion where sharpening is critical.

DIFFICULTY LEVEL

Did You Know?

You cannot use Adobe Photoshop Elements to sharpen a poorly focused digital photo. The Unsharp Mask filter only increases the perceived sharpness of an already well-focused photo. If you want a good photo that appears "tack-sharp," you must first shoot it in focus and then apply the Unsharp Mask to get the best results.

Did You Know?

You cannot determine the best settings to use to make a photographic print when using the Unsharp Mask by examining the results on your computer screen. Although it is best to examine the effects at full image resolution when using a computer screen, you can best determine the success or failure of your settings by making a print and examining it carefully.

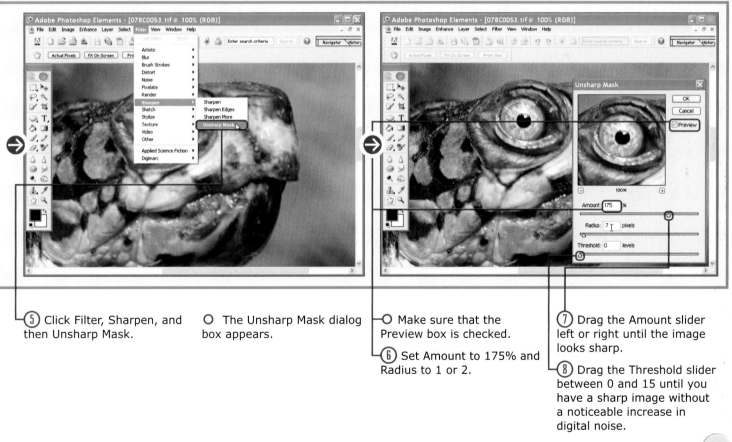

⑤ Click Filter, Sharpen, and then Unsharp Mask.

○ The Unsharp Mask dialog box appears.

○ Make sure that the Preview box is checked.

⑥ Set Amount to 175% and Radius to 1 or 2.

⑦ Drag the Amount slider left or right until the image looks sharp.

⑧ Drag the Threshold slider between 0 and 15 until you have a sharp image without a noticeable increase in digital noise.

PRECISELY POSITION PHOTOS
on a page

You may have many reasons to precisely position one or more photos on a page. Maybe you want to create your own print portfolio, a scrapbook page, or a greeting card. Whatever the reason, you can take several approaches. Depending on the printer you use, your printer software may have a feature that enables you to specify exactly where an image should be printed on the page. If you are only printing a page with one photo, using your printer software may be the best approach.

You can use Adobe Photoshop Elements' Image, Resize, Canvas Size command to "add paper" around an open image when you want only a single photo on a page. To use this feature, you need to calculate the amount of paper to add to each side. Or, you can create a new blank page and drag and drop one or more open photos onto the new page and place them where you want using the Ruler feature.

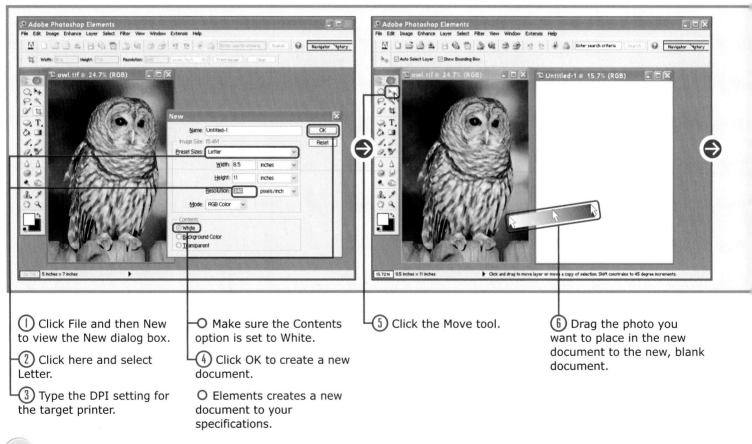

① Click File and then New to view the New dialog box.

② Click here and select Letter.

③ Type the DPI setting for the target printer.

─○ Make sure the Contents option is set to White.

④ Click OK to create a new document.

○ Elements creates a new document to your specifications.

⑤ Click the Move tool.

⑥ Drag the photo you want to place in the new document to the new, blank document.

#87

Did You Know?

When you drag and drop, or when you cut and paste one image into a blank page, the images are all placed on their own layers. To view and select these layers, open the Layers palette. You can easily add any one of many varieties of drop shadows or other effects by simply opening the Layer Styles palette and double-clicking the style of your choice.

Did You Know?

Each time you place a new image on a page as a layer, you increase the size of the file. To flatten the layers, click Layer and then Flatten Image from the menu. Save the file as a PSD file if you want to save the layers for future editing.

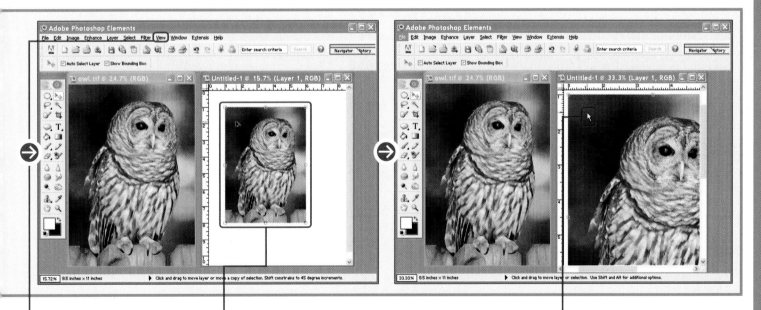

⑦ Click View.

⑧ Click Rulers.

○ The rulers appear in the new document window.

⑨ Click the photo layer with the Move tool to move the image where you want it.

○ If you click and drag on the handles around the photo, you can change the size of the image. Press Shift while dragging to maintain the aspect ratio.

⑩ Press Ctrl + (plus sign) to increase zoom, or Ctrl – (minus sign) to decrease zoom so that you have a larger and more precise ruler.

⑪ Drag the photo with the Move tool until you have the image positioned as you want it.

○ You can move the image up and down and sideways by tapping on the arrow keys. Each tap moves the image one pixel.

PRINT MULTIPLE PHOTOS

on a page

You can save photo paper, printer ink, and money by creating a multi-photo layout and printing more than one photo per page. Although you can do this manually by using several of the features found in Adobe Photoshop Elements, the Picture Package feature lets you quickly and easily make multi-photo prints that are similar to school photo pages.

Besides using one of the 20 preformatted pages, you can also customize your own layout. You can learn

more about making customized layouts by consulting Adobe Photoshop Elements' Help system. You can also automatically make a multi-photo print of every photo in a selected folder. The Picture Package's default layout is for multiple copies of a single photo. After you have selected a layout, however, you can click each photo and pick another photo to fill that space.

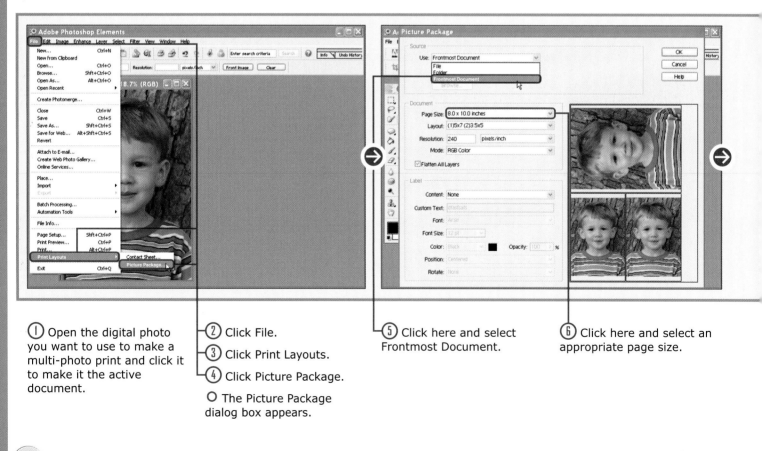

① Open the digital photo you want to use to make a multi-photo print and click it to make it the active document.

② Click File.

③ Click Print Layouts.

④ Click Picture Package.

○ The Picture Package dialog box appears.

⑤ Click here and select Frontmost Document.

⑥ Click here and select an appropriate page size.

88

Did You Know?

When you want a multi-photo layout made of more than one photo, you can place all of the selected photos into a folder and set the Source to the selected folder. The Picture Package feature automatically creates one page featuring multiple photos of each of the selected photos in the chosen format.

Did You Know?

You can use Adobe Photoshop Elements' Picture Package feature to create multi-photo layouts and then have them printed using an online photo-printing service such as Shutterfly. See task #90 to learn more about Shutterfly's services.

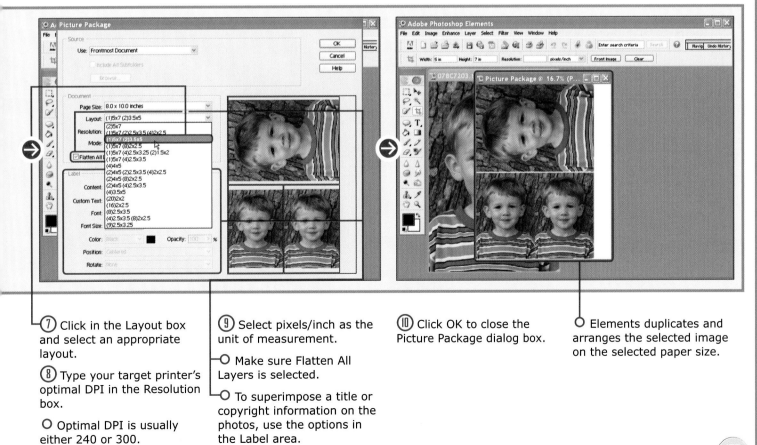

⑦ Click in the Layout box and select an appropriate layout.

⑧ Type your target printer's optimal DPI in the Resolution box.

○ Optimal DPI is usually either 240 or 300.

⑨ Select pixels/inch as the unit of measurement.

○ Make sure Flatten All Layers is selected.

○ To superimpose a title or copyright information on the photos, use the options in the Label area.

⑩ Click OK to close the Picture Package dialog box.

○ Elements duplicates and arranges the selected image on the selected paper size.

THUMBNAILS

The more digital photographs you take, the more likely you are to need thumbnail images for reference and archiving purposes. Adobe Photoshop Elements' Contact Sheet feature is an excellent tool to use to automatically create thumbnail images on one or more pages and in a useful size for your needs.

Besides being able to create thumbnail image pages to place in three-ring binders, you can also make thumbnail image pages to use on CD-ROM or

DVD-ROM cases, or for viewing on a computer screen, or for displaying in a Web page as a single graphic image. After choosing one or more folders of images, Adobe Photoshop Element's Contact Sheet automatically creates the thumbnail images and places them on one or more pages with filenames if desired.

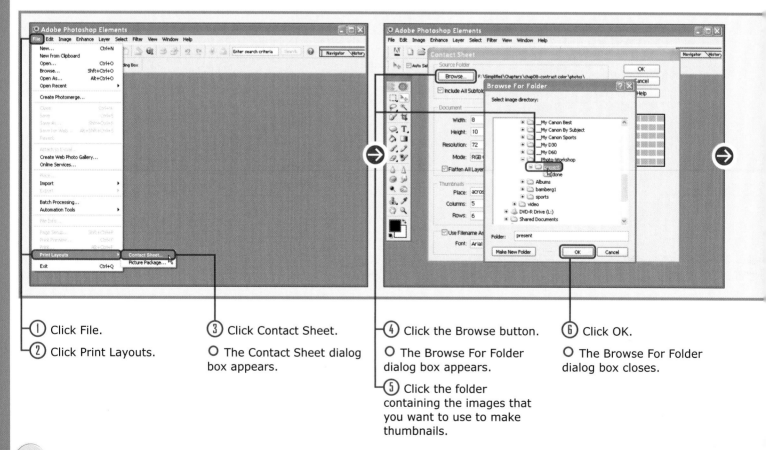

① Click File.

② Click Print Layouts.

③ Click Contact Sheet.

O The Contact Sheet dialog box appears.

④ Click the Browse button.

O The Browse For Folder dialog box appears.

⑤ Click the folder containing the images that you want to use to make thumbnails.

⑥ Click OK.

O The Browse For Folder dialog box closes.

Did You Know?

Did You Know?

When you need to share a large number of images with someone via e-mail, you can use Adobe Photoshop Elements' Contact Sheet feature to create screen-resolution size thumbnail images with as many as 25 or more thumbnails per 800 x 600-pixel image that are under 75K is size.

#89

DIFFICULTY LEVEL

Did You Know?

Adobe Photoshop Elements' Contact Sheet feature is a good tool to use to make an index for a scrapbook or photo portfolio. After you have created the page, you can further enhance the page with borders, headings, and other textual information. You can even rearrange the thumbnail images if you remove the check mark from the Flatten All Layers box.

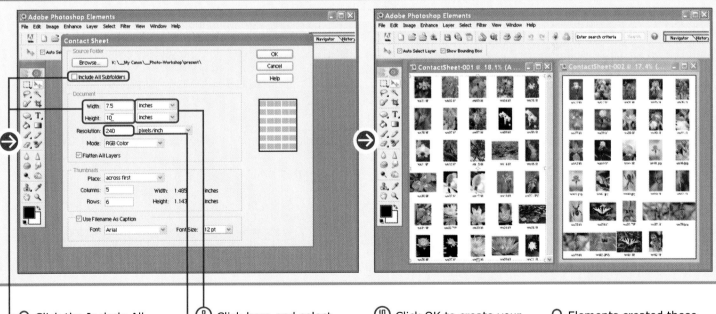

─O Click the Include All Subfolders check box if you want to make thumbnails in the subfolders.

⑦ Type **7.5** in the Width box and **10** in the Height box to make an 8½" x 11" page.

⑧ Click here and select inches.

⑨ Type your printer's optimal DPI (typically 240 or 300).

O Make sure the Flatten All Layers check box is selected.

⑩ Click OK to create your contact sheet of thumbnail images.

O Elements created these two pages of thumbnail images to be printed on 8½" x 11" paper with three-ring binder holes.

Order prints
ONLINE

If you enjoy using a one-hour photo-finishing service at a local photo lab, you may enjoy using one of the online printing services such as Shutterfly. Although it is not possible to get your photo prints back in an hour, you can select, edit, upload, and order photo prints from your computer any time you like without the hassles of going to a local lab to drop off your photos and to pick them up. After uploading your photos to an online printing service, your photos are printed and delivered to your mailbox within a few days.

Besides being able to order prints for yourself after you have uploaded them, you can also send a link via e-mail to anyone else that you want to share them with. They can view the photos online in a Web browser; if they want, they can order prints themselves at their own expense or you can order prints to mail to them. Besides just ordering photo prints at competitive prices, your photos can also be printed in photo albums, on hats, on greeting cards, calendars, and many other photo gift items.

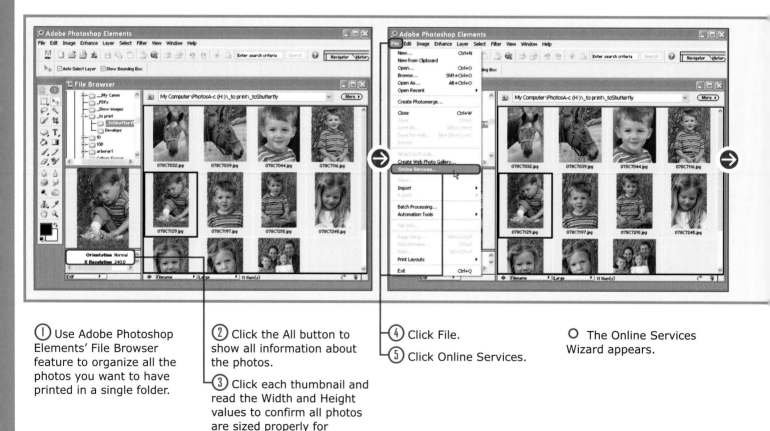

① Use Adobe Photoshop Elements' File Browser feature to organize all the photos you want to have printed in a single folder.

② Click the All button to show all information about the photos.

③ Click each thumbnail and read the Width and Height values to confirm all photos are sized properly for uploading.

④ Click File.

⑤ Click Online Services.

○ The Online Services Wizard appears.

Did You Know?

The best way to use an
online photo printing service is
to crop, edit, and place all the
photos you want into a single folder
before uploading to an online photo-
printing service. Crop each of these photos
to the aspect ratio of the print size you will
want to order and save them in the JPEG file
format.

Did You Know?

You can enter the e-mail and mailing
addresses for people who you want to share
your photos with. You can even import your
addresses from Microsoft Outlook or Palm Desktop.
This makes it easy to share your photos or to order
prints and have them sent to friends or family without
having to enter addresses.

#90

DIFFICULTY LEVEL

CONTINUED ▶

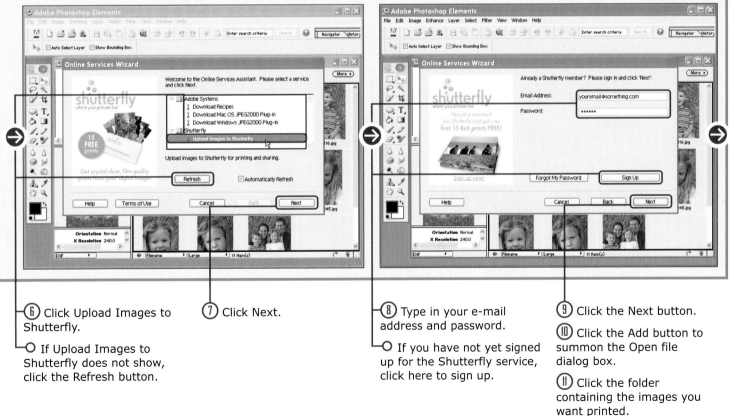

⑥ Click Upload Images to
Shutterfly.

○ If Upload Images to
Shutterfly does not show,
click the Refresh button.

⑦ Click Next.

⑧ Type in your e-mail
address and password.

○ If you have not yet signed
up for the Shutterfly service,
click here to sign up.

⑨ Click the Next button.

⑩ Click the Add button to
summon the Open file
dialog box.

⑪ Click the folder
containing the images you
want printed.

Order prints
ONLINE

Shutterfly provides four different ways for you to upload your digital photos. You can use the built-in link found on Adobe Photoshop Elements' Online Services Wizard, download and use the free Shutterfly SmartUpload software from www.shutterfly.com, use the Picture Upload plug-in in your Internet browser, or add the pictures you want one-by-one through your Web browser. If you upload and order online often, your best choice is the Shutterfly SmartUpload software.

Some of the more fun ways to present your photos when ordering online from Shutterfly is in a *Snapbook.*

Snapbooks are 4" x 6" and 5" x 7" mini-albums protected in a clear matte finish cover and bound with a clear spiral binding. When you order a Snapbook, you can also add captions for each photo and choose from a variety of styles including classic, elegant, or fun. Each style describes a layout, a page design, and text type.

Shutterfly also offers photo calendars. Besides picking a photo for each month, you can also choose the starting month, the cover photo, and a cover title. The calendars cost around $20.

CONTINUED ▶

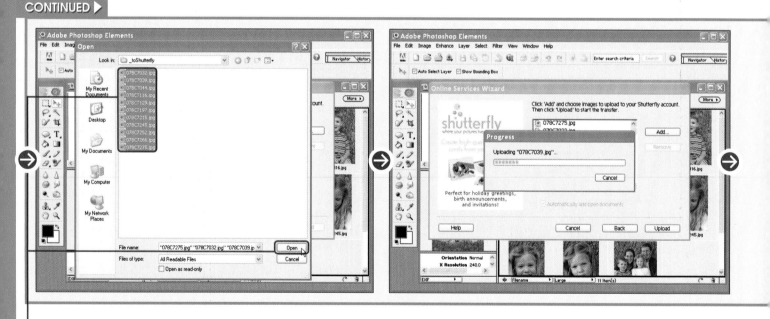

⑫ Select the image files you want.

⑬ Click Open to return to the Online Services Wizard.

⑭ Click Upload to begin uploading your images into an album.

○ The Progress bar indicates which photo is uploading and how much of the file still remains to upload.

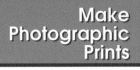
Did You Know?

Other online photo-printing services you may want to consider in addition to Shutterfly (www.shutterfly.com) are ezprints (www.ezprints.com), ImageStation (www.imagestation.com), and Ofoto (www.ofoto.com).

If you are using a Mac, you can upload and order photo prints and photo books easily by using Apple's iPhoto 2 photo application or any of the other online photo-processing services that enable you to upload via a Web browser.

Did You Know?

Several online photo-printing services including Shutterfly offer "pro" photo printing services that allow you to set prices for your photos and have your customers view and order photos directly from a Web site. This allows you to simply shoot photos and receive money for them without all the hassles of taking orders, making or ordering prints, and delivering them.

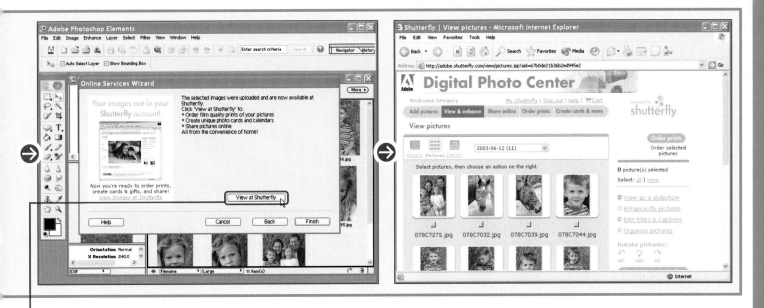

⑮ Click View at Shutterfly to visit the Shutterfly Web site.

○ This Shutterfly page enables you to order prints of the uploaded photos.

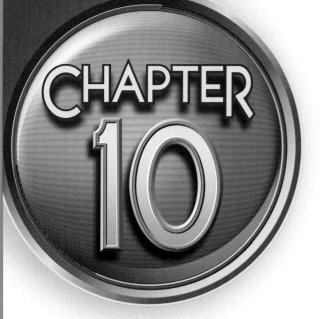

CHAPTER 10

Digital Photo Projects

After you have taken a few good photos and edited them, you are ready to use your photos in digital photo projects. Two good digital photo projects to start with are to organize your digital photo collection with an image manager and to archive your valuable digital photo collection to external hard drives or offline storage media, such as a CD or DVD. After you have organized and archived your digital photo collection, you are ready to complete more digital photo projects.

One of the most exciting aspects of digital photography is that you can easily share and enjoy your digital photos in many ways. You can attach one or more photos to e-mail, create slideshows to show on your computer screen or even on a TV screen, publish online photo galleries, create digital photo albums, make collages, and more.

Many digital photo projects require software and hardware beyond what you use to import and edit photos. With increased interest in digital photography, the marketplace offers an incredible number of products from which to choose. Often you can choose one software product that allows you to complete most or all of your projects. Some of the more feature-rich and easy-to-use products include Adobe Photoshop Album (www.adobe.com), Adobe Photoshop Elements (www.adobe.com), Apple iPhoto (www.apple.com), Jasc Software Paint Photo Album (www.jascsoftware .com), Roxio Easy CD & DVD Creator (www.roxio.com), Roxio PhotoSuite Platinum Edition (www.roxio.com), Ulead DVD Picture Show (www.ulead.com), and Ulead Explorer (www.ulead.com).

TOP 100

ORGANIZE
your digital photos

After you have stored a few hundred of your digital photos on your computer, you will need an effective way to organize and manage your growing digital photo collection. Software products that allow you to easily manage large digital photo collections are called *image managers,* and there are a number of good ones available. One of the more powerful and easy-to-use image managers is Cerious Software's ThumbsPlus, which you can download from www.cerious.com.

After you pick one or more folders or drives to manage, ThumbsPlus automatically creates thumbnail

images for every digital photo file in the selected folders or drives. You can view the images quickly by looking at the thumbnails, and also view a variety of textual information, such as the EXIF data that image files may contain. To learn more about working with EXIF date, see task #17.

The ThumbsPlus database not only keeps a database of the filenames and thumbnail images but also acts as a repository for a variety of other useful textual information. You can add keywords to photos, save location information, add annotations and copyright information, and more.

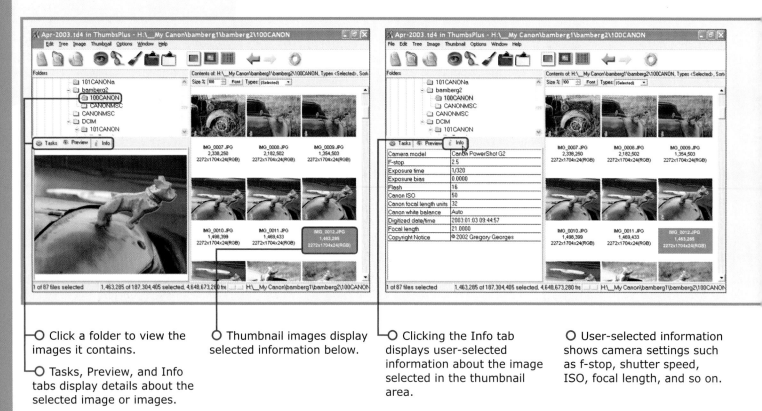

O Click a folder to view the images it contains.

O Tasks, Preview, and Info tabs display details about the selected image or images.

O Thumbnail images display selected information below.

O Clicking the Info tab displays user-selected information about the image selected in the thumbnail area.

O User-selected information shows camera settings such as f-stop, shutter speed, ISO, focal length, and so on.

Did You Know? ※

ThumbsPlus offers many features for viewing digital photos. Besides being able to scale the thumbnails and view more or fewer of them at a time, you can also choose a list or report view, which you can customize to show just the textual information you want. You can open more than one copy of ThumbsPlus at a time. This enables you to drag and drop photos from one folder into another folder while viewing the contents of each folder.

Did You Know? ※

When you want to carefully compare one or more digital photos side by side, you can choose View Synched. The synch view allows you to scroll one image while the other images are simultaneously scrolled.

CONTINUED ▶

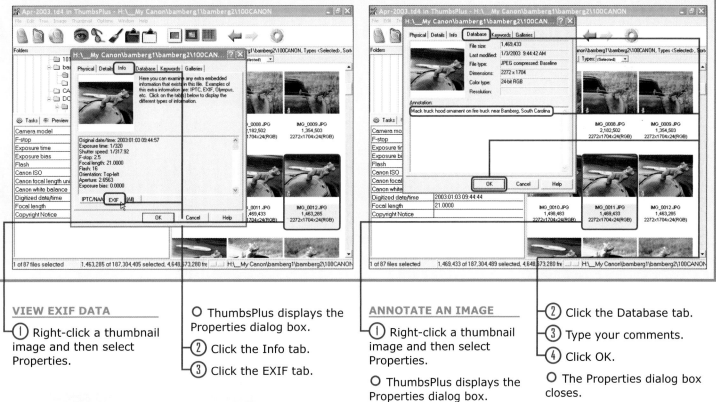

VIEW EXIF DATA

① Right-click a thumbnail image and then select Properties.

○ ThumbsPlus displays the Properties dialog box.

② Click the Info tab.

③ Click the EXIF tab.

ANNOTATE AN IMAGE

① Right-click a thumbnail image and then select Properties.

○ ThumbsPlus displays the Properties dialog box.

② Click the Database tab.

③ Type your comments.

④ Click OK.

○ The Properties dialog box closes.

ORGANIZE
your digital photos

Many software vendors who initially created image managers have realized the value of adding features that increase your ability to organize and manage your digital photo collection. They have also added a considerable number of project features such as slideshows, Web galleries, contact sheets, printed image catalogs, and much more. In addition to ThumbsPlus, a few of the more feature-rich and easy-to-use image managers with useful project features are:

ACDSee 5.0 (www.acdsystems.com)

Adobe Photoshop Album (www.adobe.com)

Apple iPhoto 2 (www.apple.com)

Cerious Software ThumbsPlus 6.0 (www.cerious.com)

Jasc Software Paint Photo Album 4.0 (www.jascsoftware.com)

Ulead Explorer (www.ulead.com)

Also consider using some of the digital photo tools included with your operating system. Windows XP, Windows 2000, and Mac OS X offer a number of useful features such as View Thumbnails, Photo Printing Wizard, and Slide Show.

CONTINUED ▶

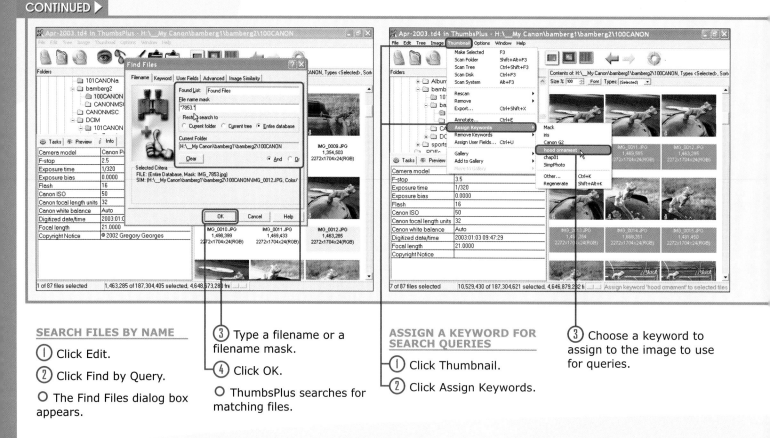

SEARCH FILES BY NAME

① Click Edit.

② Click Find by Query.

○ The Find Files dialog box appears.

③ Type a filename or a filename mask.

④ Click OK.

○ ThumbsPlus searches for matching files.

ASSIGN A KEYWORD FOR SEARCH QUERIES

① Click Thumbnail.

② Click Assign Keywords.

③ Choose a keyword to assign to the image to use for queries.

91
CONTINUED

Did You Know? ※

One of the most useful features found in ThumbsPlus is the Edit➪Find Similar Images command. You can use this command to find images that look similar based upon a number of metrics, including color and image shape.

Did You Know? ※

You can automatically rename a batch of your digital photo files using the ThumbsPlus Automatic File Rename command. You can choose a prefix and a suffix as well as add incrementing numbers. This useful feature allows you to add more meaning to your filenames. You can also set the filename to be automatically used as a keyword, enabling you to perform keyword queries using just parts of the filename.

CONTINUED ▶

FIND AN IMAGE CONTAINING KEYWORDS

① Click Edit.

② Click Find by Query.

○ The Find Files dialog box appears.

③ Click the Keyword tab.

④ Type keywords, separated by commas.

⑤ Click OK.

○ A window displays all images with the selected keywords.

FIND A SIMILAR-LOOKING IMAGE

① Click Edit.

② Click Find Similar Images.

○ The Find Files dialog box appears.

③ Click the Image Similarity tab.

④ Specify similarity settings here.

⑤ Click OK to display a folder with similar images in the Found Files folder.

ORGANIZE
your digital photos

One of the greatest challenges is to manage digital photos that are stored on multiple drives, on networks, and on removable media all from the same image manager and to have all the images accessible at the same time. Using ThumbsPlus, you can manage images on multiple drives on one PC, or one or more drives on some networks.

You can also create thumbnail images and build ThumbsPlus database information on digital photos stored on removable media and external drives. When you remove an external drive, the thumbnails

and database information remain inside the Offline Disks folder. Likewise, you can create thumbnail images and database information for digital photos on a CD-ROM. When the CD-ROM is not in the drive, you can view the thumbnails and database information in the Offline CD-ROMs folder.

As the storage requirements for digital photographers grow, these features become more useful for managing, organizing, and archiving digital photos on a variety of drives and media.

CONTINUED ▶

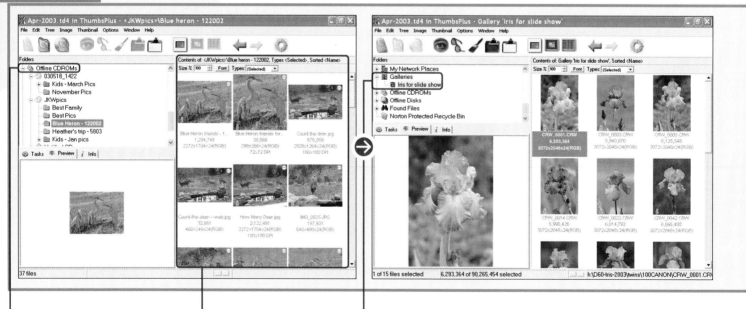

VIEW FILES IN OFFLINE STORAGE

○ After creating thumbnails for removable media such as a CD-ROM, ThumbsPlus saves the thumbnails and associated information in the Offline CDROMs folder.

○ You can view thumbnails for offline media without inserting the media in a drive.

○ Galleries are logical containers that contain thumbnails stored in a database, but not the full images themselves.

#91 CONTINUED

Did You Know? ※

The ThumbsPlus Gallery feature enables you to save disk space while being able to view thumbnails of the same digital photo in multiple folders. For example, you can save all of the digital photos from a trip to Europe in a single folder. You can then create separate gallery folders for landscapes, cities, seascapes, and castles. By right-clicking a group of landscape photos in the Europe folder, you can add them to the landscape gallery. You can do the same for all the city, seascape, and castle photos in the Europe folder. This lets you open a single folder and view all of the thumbnails for a single subject no matter what folder contains the original digital photo file — all while having only a single copy of the file.

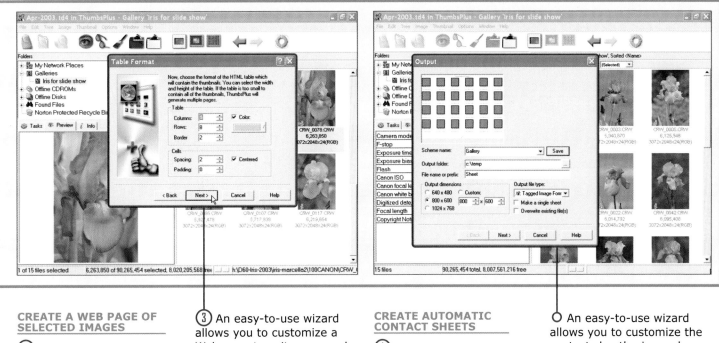

CREATE A WEB PAGE OF SELECTED IMAGES

① Click Image.

② Click Web Page Wizard.

③ An easy-to-use wizard allows you to customize a Web page to suit your needs.

CREATE AUTOMATIC CONTACT SHEETS

① Click Image.

② Click Contact Sheets.

○ An easy-to-use wizard allows you to customize the contact sheet's size and layout to suit your needs.

Share digital photos with
AOL INSTANT MESSENGER

Instant messengers (*IMs*) are software applications that enable you to exchange text messages in real time with other people on the Internet who have compatible IM software. As soon as you type a message and click the Send button, the message displays on the screen of those with whom you are chatting. They can then type a message and send a reply back to you. IMs allow a much more interactive way to communicate than the slower e-mail. You can also create a chat room where you can invite multiple people to join in the chat.

Besides messaging capability, many of the more popular IMs have features that enable you to send a file, which means that you can easily send digital photo files. Sharing your digital photos while chatting about them is a wonderful way to not only share your photos with others, but for you to get feedback.

Although AOL's Instant Messenger is one of the more popular IMs, you can use other versions like ICQ (www.icq.com) and MSN Messenger (www.microsoft.com).

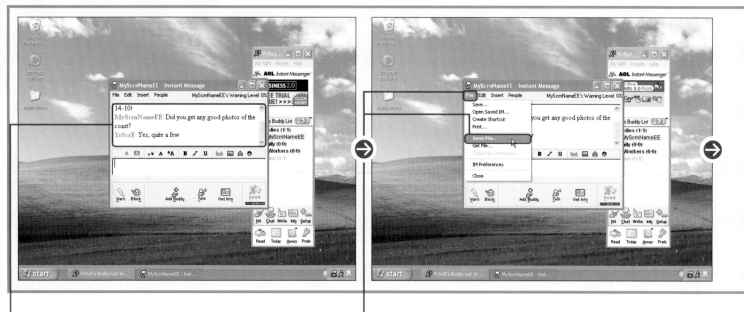

① Sign in and initiate a chat with a buddy.

② Click File.

③ Click Send File.

○ The Send File dialog box appears.

#92

DIFFICULTY LEVEL

Did You Know? ☼

AOL Instant Messenger is available for those who have paid for and have subscribed to the AOL service. AOL also offers a free version that is available to non-AOL subscribers. You can download the free version from the AOL Web site (www.aol.com). After downloading the software, you can install it, register a screen name, and be chatting within a few minutes.

Caution! ☼

You should be careful who you accept digital photos from while chatting; you may accept and view a file that you would rather not have seen. The Preferences dialog box offers options to prevent others from sending you digital photos unless you accept them.

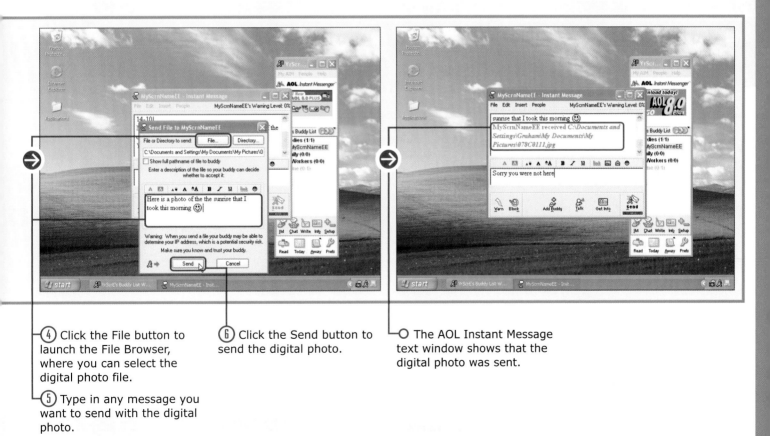

④ Click the File button to launch the File Browser, where you can select the digital photo file.

⑤ Type in any message you want to send with the digital photo.

⑥ Click the Send button to send the digital photo.

○ The AOL Instant Message text window shows that the digital photo was sent.

ARCHIVE
your digital photo collection to a DVD-ROM

Occasionally a hard drive fails. The older your hard drive is, the more likely it is to fail. To avoid losing all or part of your digital photo collection, you should keep your photos well organized with an image manager and have a procedure in place for periodically archiving (copying) them to another hard drive or to removable media such as a CD-ROM or DVD-ROM.

One of the easiest and safest ways to archive your digital photos is to burn (write) them to a DVD-ROM. To do that you need a *DVD burner* — a DVD drive

that both reads and writes DVD discs — and software to manage the process. One excellent software product for archiving digital photos to a DVD-ROM is Roxio Easy CD & DVD Creator, a feature-rich product that enables you to easily archive just a few files or many files that require multiple DVD discs. It also comes with software for printing disc labels and jewel and DVD case inserts.

Turn to task #91 for more on how to organize your photos with an image manager.

① Click the drive and folder containing the files you want to archive.

② Click the Data tab to select record mode.

Did You Know? ☀

A DVD-ROM holds 4.7GB of
digital photos or slightly more
than seven CD-ROMs. Using a 3-
megapixel camera to shoot in the RAW
format, you can archive around 1,500 digital
photos or the equivalent of around 40 rolls of
36-exposure film on a single DVD-ROM disc.

#93

DIFFICULTY LEVEL

Caution! ☀

Because it is not certain how long a DVD disc will safely
store your digital photos and because a single
scratch can prevent you from retrieving your
photos, you should take all precautions to protect
your archives. Purchasing two different brands of
quality DVD discs and making two copies when you
archive your photos — using one of each brand — is
wise. This procedure may prevent you losing photos
on defective media.

CONTINUED ▶

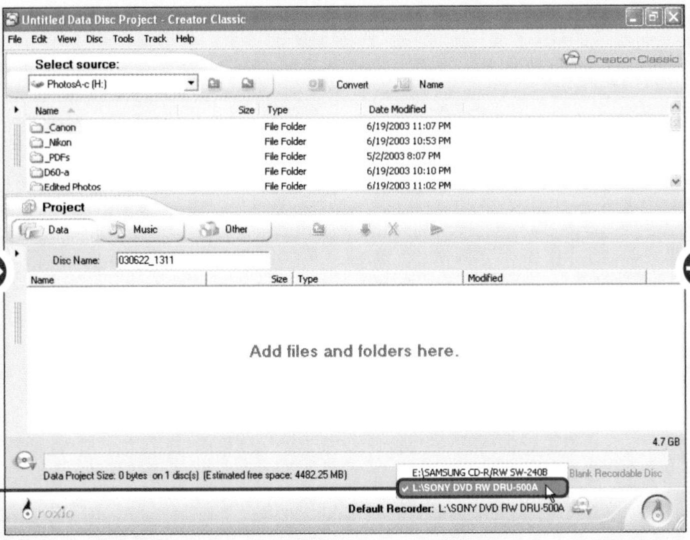

③ Click the Default
Recorder icon to select
the DVD drive.

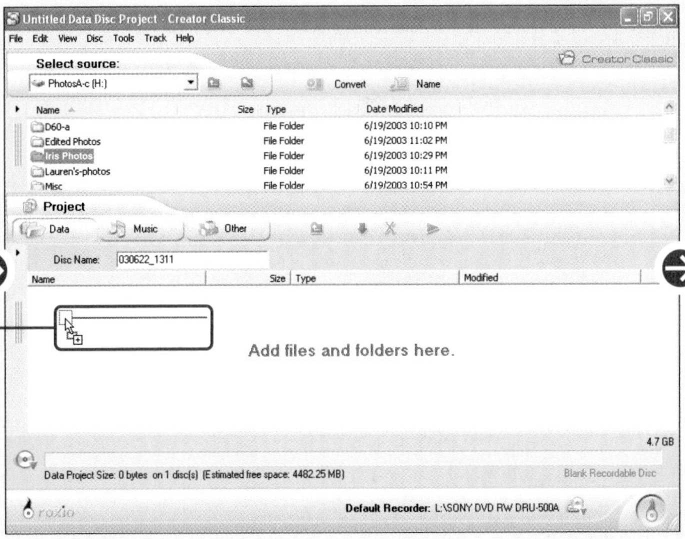

④ Drag one or more folders
or files from the Source
Window to the Project
Window.

ARCHIVE
your digital photo collection to a DVD-ROM

When choosing a DVD burner and DVD discs, you must be careful to choose the right format. What is the right format? Unfortunately, drive and media manufacturers are engaged in a standards war, so multiple competing formats exist in the marketplace. Some of the more common formats include DVD-R, DVD+R, DVD-RW, and DVD+RW; then there are also DVD-Video and DVD-RAM.

When choosing a format to archive your digital photographs, you may want to make sure you choose a drive that will allow you to write digital

video slide shows to view on your computer or TV screen. Several manufacturers are making the choice easier by offering DVD burners that can write in multiple formats. To learn about creating a slideshow to view on a DVD player, see task #97.

Even though there are competing DVD formats, there is not a good reason *not* to buy a DVD burner for archiving your digital photographs. DVD burners are currently one of the best ways to archive your digital photos for safekeeping because of the number of digital photos you can store on a DVD.

CONTINUED ▶

—O The Disc Info bar shows how many discs are needed and the available space.

—O Large digital photo collections may be archived to more than one disk.

—O Clicking a folder or file and then clicking the Remove from Project button removes folders or files from the list of items to be copied.

⑤ Click the Record button.

O The Record Setup dialog box appears.

Caution! ※

Some early DVD drives and DVD-burning software may write to discs in a format that cannot be read by some of the more current DVD drives. Be careful to use a DVD drive and software that will allow you to read your discs in new DVD drives and on computers with current operating systems.

Did You Know? ※

DVD drives require firmware and a driver. If you are having problems with your DVD drive, you should check the vendor's Web site for new drivers or firmware. Vendors usually provide easy-to-follow instructions for downloading and installing both the drivers and firmware. When downloading the drivers, be sure to select the correct one for your operating system.

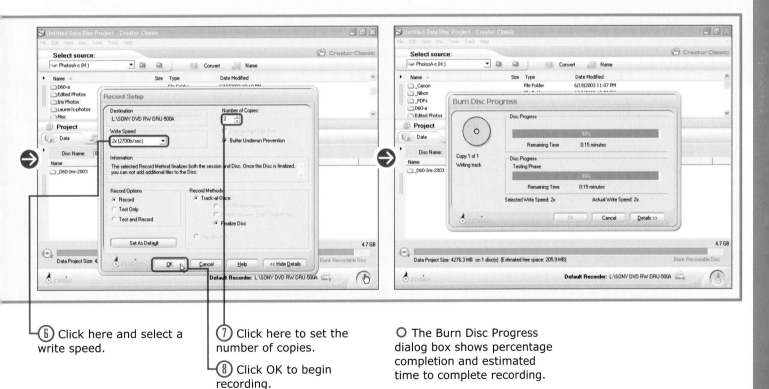

⑥ Click here and select a write speed.

⑦ Click here to set the number of copies.

⑧ Click OK to begin recording.

○ The Burn Disc Progress dialog box shows percentage completion and estimated time to complete recording.

Create a
PDF SLIDESHOW

One of the more fun ways to share photos is to create and view them in a slideshow on a computer screen. You can use many applications to create slide shows. Adobe Photoshop Elements enables you to quickly and easily create a PDF slideshow. A *PDF* (*Portable Document Format*) is a special file that can only be read using Adobe Acrobat or the free Adobe Acrobat Reader. You can view PDF files on just about all computers, including PC and Mac. So, you can create a slideshow using a PC or Mac and share it

with anyone no matter what computer he or she is using.

After you have created a PDF slideshow, all the photos and the settings you selected for playback are all contained in a single file. One of the significant advantages to sharing your digital photos in PDF format is that there are a number of useful features built-in to the Acrobat Reader that allow the images to be exported, edited, printed, and so on.

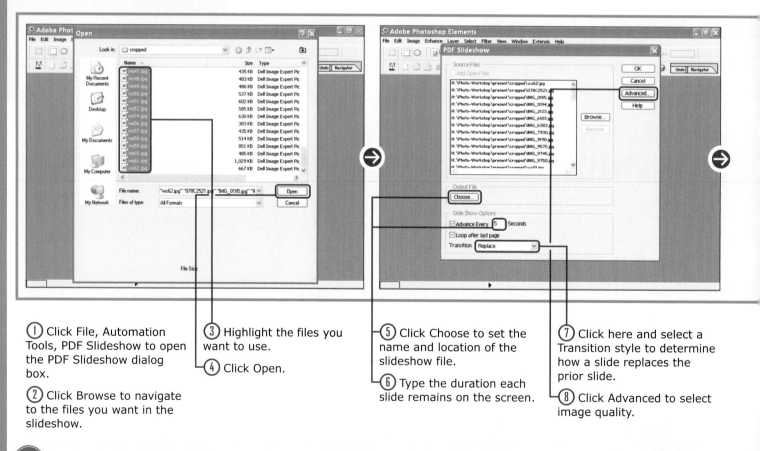

① Click File, Automation Tools, PDF Slideshow to open the PDF Slideshow dialog box.

② Click Browse to navigate to the files you want in the slideshow.

③ Highlight the files you want to use.

④ Click Open.

⑤ Click Choose to set the name and location of the slideshow file.

⑥ Type the duration each slide remains on the screen.

⑦ Click here and select a Transition style to determine how a slide replaces the prior slide.

⑧ Click Advanced to select image quality.

Did You Know? ※

To view Acrobat slideshows created with Adobe Photoshop Elements, you need a copy of Adobe Acrobat or a copy of the free Acrobat Reader. You can download a free copy of Adobe Acrobat Reader 6.0 at:

www.adobe.com/products/acrobat/readermain.html

When using Acrobat Reader 6.0, you can easily export pictures, edit pictures, print pictures, order prints online, and order photo objects online by simply clicking on the Picture Tasks button in Acrobat Reader 6.0.

Did You Know? ※

In addition to Acrobat Reader, Adobe also offers Adobe Acrobat, a feature-rich application used to create, view, and edit PDF files. If you want to add text and lines directly on a digital photo, then Acrobat is an excellent product to use.

#94

DIFFICULTY LEVEL

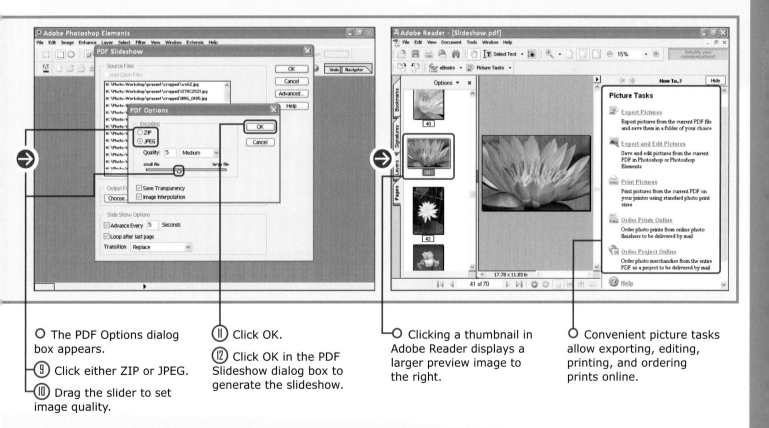

○ The PDF Options dialog box appears.

⑨ Click either ZIP or JPEG.

⑩ Drag the slider to set image quality.

⑪ Click OK.

⑫ Click OK in the PDF Slideshow dialog box to generate the slideshow.

─○ Clicking a thumbnail in Adobe Reader displays a larger preview image to the right.

○ Convenient picture tasks allow exporting, editing, printing, and ordering prints online.

Create a
DIGITAL PHOTO ALBUM

You can create the digital equivalent of a photo album with realistic flipping pages with one of E-Book Systems's FlipAlbum products, available at www.flipalbum.com. You can choose from multiple versions of FlipAlbum. FlipAlbum 5 Standard automatically organizes your photos into realistic page-flipping albums that you can view on a PC and share on the Internet. FlipAlbum 5 Suite has extra features that enable you to share your albums on CDs or to play them on some DVD players. FlipAlbum Pro offers all the features of the other two products plus a few more features, including a CD password option,

image encryption, watermark capabilities, and a print lock feature to control how images are printed. Mac FlipAlbum 3 is for a Mac.

To create an album, you simply select Folder⇒Open Folder and select a folder of images. FlipAlbum then automatically creates a front and back cover, thumbnail image pages to be used as a table of contents, and an index. Image viewing can be ordered based upon the filenames, or you can click and drag the thumbnail images to order them as you want them.

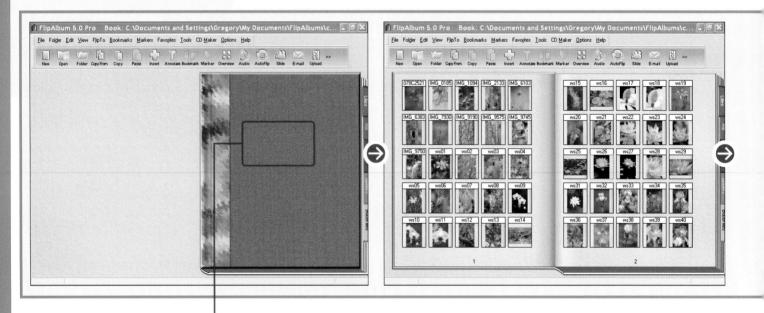

○ After selecting Folder, Open Folder, and selecting a folder of photos, FlipAlbum automatically creates a flip album based upon default settings.

○ The Cover title text was added with the Annotations tool.

○ Thumbnails are automatically generated and placed at the front of an album.

○ To set image viewing order, click and drag and drop the thumbnails in the order you want.

○ To view a full-size image on an album page, click its thumbnail.

#95

DIFFICULTY LEVEL

Did You Know? ※

You can further customize a FlipAlbum by selecting a different cover style or by choosing your own cover color, cover image, texture, and binding. You can also choose the color and texture of the pages, the margins, and how the pages "flip." You can add background music and set the entire album to flip automatically. You can add text to each page in a font style and color of your choice, and you can add even add a link to a specified Web page.

Apply It! ※

You can upload your FlipAlbums to E-Book Systems's Web site specifically for sharing FlipAlbums at www.fliplibrary.com.

○ To add a tab, right-click the selected page, choose Bookmarks, Add, and then type in the tab text and choose a color.

○ To turn a page, click in the upper corner of a page to view a flipping page effect.

○ FlipAlbum automatically creates clickable indexes at the end of each album when a folder is opened.

Create a
WEB PHOTO GALLERY

If you want to make your photos available to anyone in the world who has a computer and a connection to the Internet, you can create an online photo gallery. To create an online photo gallery, you typically need digital photos sized and optimized for use on the Internet, thumbnail images sized and optimized for use on the Internet, and HTML-based pages (Web pages) with links to the digital photos, thumbnails, and HTML pages. Creating all of this without a tool like Adobe Photoshop Elements is a tedious and time-consuming process.

Using Adobe Photoshop Elements' Create Web Gallery feature, you can have your online gallery up and running in just a few minutes. Before you run the Create Web Gallery feature, you should first prepare your digital photos and create a folder to put all the images and Web pages that Elements creates. Although you can use Create Web Gallery to automatically size and compress each digital photo, you may get better results sizing and compressing each digital photo with the Save for Web command (see task #71).

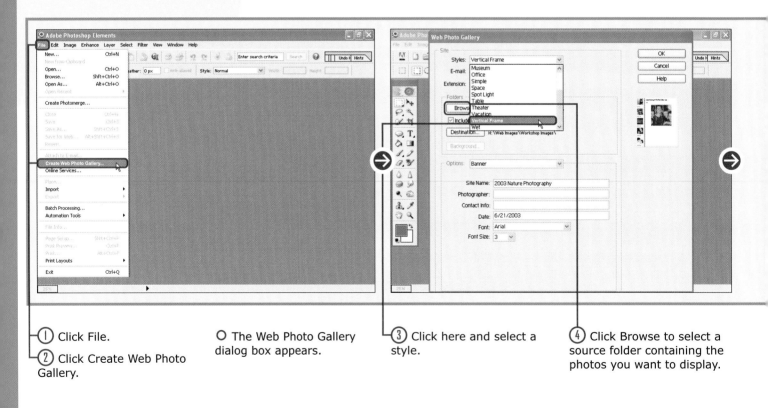

① Click File.

② Click Create Web Photo Gallery.

O The Web Photo Gallery dialog box appears.

③ Click here and select a style.

④ Click Browse to select a source folder containing the photos you want to display.

Did You Know? ※

Most Internet service providers offer you 10MB or more of personal Web space that you can use for your digital photo gallery. Check with your service provider to learn more about the file transfer tools they offer and how to upload your digital photo gallery. Often you can find this information on your Internet service provider's Web pages.

Did You Know? ※

Adobe Photoshop Elements' Create Web Photo Gallery can automatically place a caption under each photo on each Web page. Use the File, File Info command to add a caption in the Caption box for each digital photo file.

CONTINUED ▶

⑤ Click Destination to open the Browse For Folder dialog box.

⑥ Click a drive and folder in which to save the images, thumbnails, and Web pages.

⑦ Click OK to close the Browse For Folder dialog box.

○ Type in your e-mail address if you want to display it on each Web page.

⑧ Click here and select Banner.

⑨ Type the site name here.

⑩ Type your name here.

Create a
WEB PHOTO GALLERY

Many photographers worry about having their digital photos being stolen from online photo galleries and used without payment or permission. Although this is a reasonable concern because it does happen, small digital photo files are not all that useful for most commercial purposes. If you keep all of your posted images small, with the maximum size of less than 400 pixels, you are not likely to suffer any great loss.

You can take steps to prevent an image from being copied, or you can add a copyright or watermark to

online images so that they can be tracked and identified. However, the effort it takes to add this extra protection is generally not worth it because there are ways around each different approach. If you have good reasons for not wanting your digital photos copied, you should not post them to a Web page on the Internet.

CONTINUED ▶

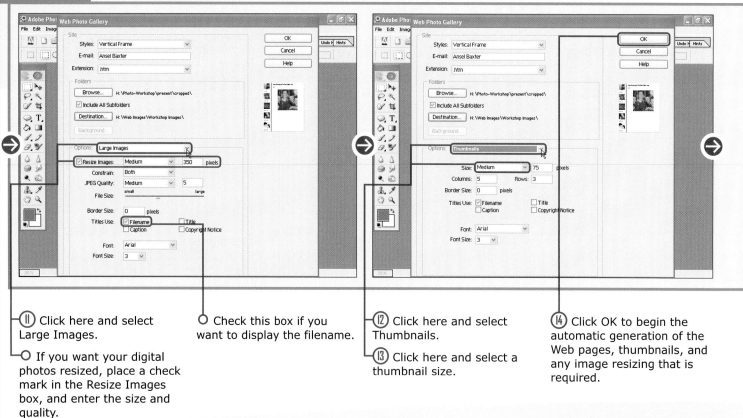

⑪ Click here and select Large Images.

○ If you want your digital photos resized, place a check mark in the Resize Images box, and enter the size and quality.

○ Check this box if you want to display the filename.

⑫ Click here and select Thumbnails.

⑬ Click here and select a thumbnail size.

⑭ Click OK to begin the automatic generation of the Web pages, thumbnails, and any image resizing that is required.

#96 CONTINUED

Did You Know? ※

GlobalSCAPE's CuteFTP (www.globalscape.com) is one of the most popular file-transfer software tools used for uploading Web pages and images to an Internet server. You can download a trial version from the vendor's Web page.

Did You Know? ※

You can change the graphics and the layout of any of the 15 preset Web page styles that are supplied with Adobe Photoshop Elements. You can find a separate folder in the /Photoshop Elements 2/Presets/WebContactSheet folder for each of the 15 styles. To modify a style, first copy the contents of the folder containing the style you want to a new folder with a different name. Then, edit or replace the images or modify the HTML code with an HTML editor.

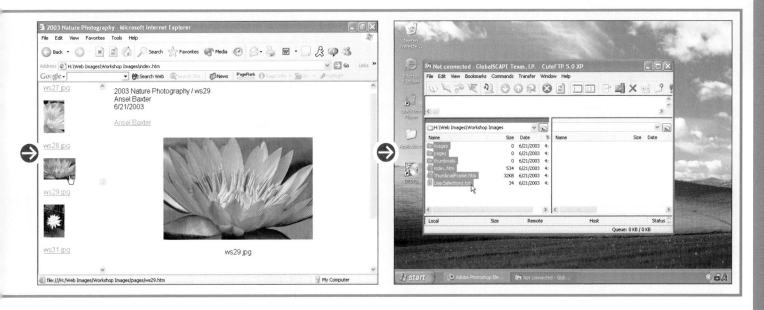

O Your Web gallery appears this way to people using Microsoft Internet Explorer.

O To upload the folders, images, and HTML-pages to the Internet, you need to use file transfer software such as Cute FTP.

Create a
VIDEO SLIDESHOW

People create slideshows for many reasons. Maybe you have just returned from an overseas trip with lots of great photos and you want to share them with friends and family. Or, maybe you have dozens of flower or antique car photos you would like to share. You may even want to create a slideshow featuring your children or your parents over the years. Whatever the reason, you can both create and present them in many ways.

One of the most useful software products to use to create slideshows on CD and DVD discs is Ulead DVD

Picture Show 2 (www.ulead.com). Using this product, you can create slideshows that you can view on a computer screen or on a TV that is connected to a DVD player *if* you have used an appropriate disc format.

An advantage of using a DVD player and a TV for viewing your slideshows is that you can control each slide with the DVD player control, which allows you to go forward or backward, or go to a main menu to select another slideshow.

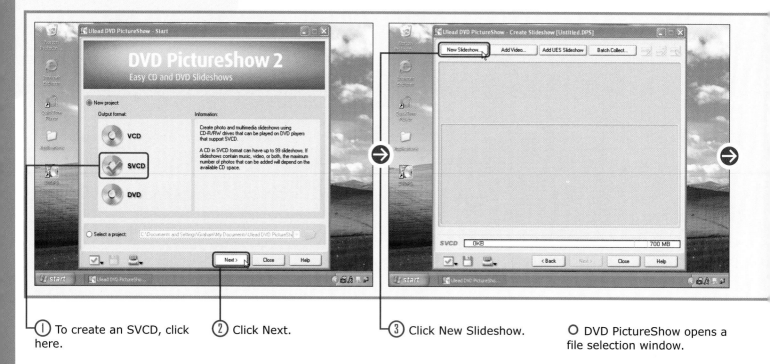

① To create an SVCD, click here.

② Click Next.

③ Click New Slideshow.

○ DVD PictureShow opens a file selection window.

#97

DIFFICULTY LEVEL

Did You Know? ※

Video CDs (VCDs) are CD-Recordable discs containing audio, video, and still images encoded in the highly-compressed MPEG (Motion Picture Experts Group) format. The VCD format offers lower-quality images than either the SVCD or DVD formats. Image resolution of full-motion video typically falls below standard VHS videotape, but still images display clearly.

Super Video CDs (SVCDs) offer better image and sound quality than VCDs, but are not as good as DVDs. However, SVCDs are a good choice for photographers because they represent an acceptable compromise between inexpensive media and high-resolution images.

A DVD is a DVD-Recordable disc that can be played in most standalone DVD players and computer DVD-ROM drives. The DVD format holds the most content and has the highest image quality.

CONTINUED ▶

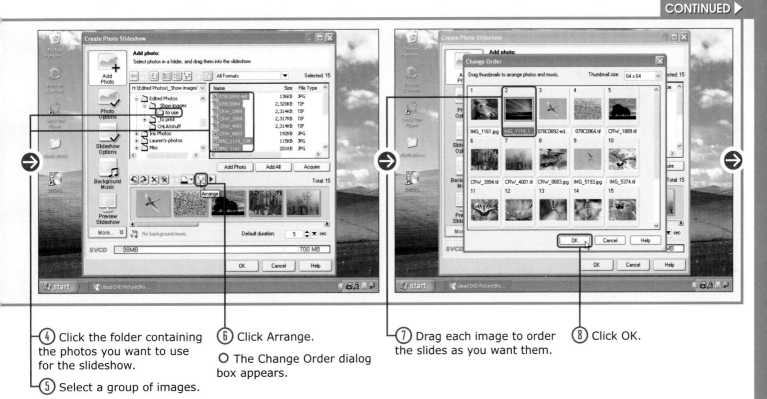

④ Click the folder containing the photos you want to use for the slideshow.

⑤ Select a group of images.

⑥ Click Arrange.

○ The Change Order dialog box appears.

⑦ Drag each image to order the slides as you want them.

⑧ Click OK.

Create a
VIDEO SLIDESHOW

Just because CD burners, DVD burners, and set-top DVD players are an evolving technology, there is no reason why you should not enjoy the benefits of this new technology now. Carefully check documentation and consult knowledgeable sales staff when purchasing new hardware and media and read the documentation that came with products you already have.

Each of the many types of discs and file formats has advantages and disadvantages. If you only have a CD burner, it is possible that you can use it to create

a VCD or SVCD featuring a photo slideshow that can be viewed on a computer with a CD-ROM reader or on a newer DVD player.

To output a DVD slideshow, you must have a DVD burner and DVD-Recordable discs (DVD-R/RWs or DVD+R/RWs). For a VCD or SVCD slideshow, you will need a CD burner and CD-R/RWs. Picking the right disc for the CD or DVD reader or set-top DVD player is as easy as reading the manuals or checking with the vendor.

CONTINUED ▶

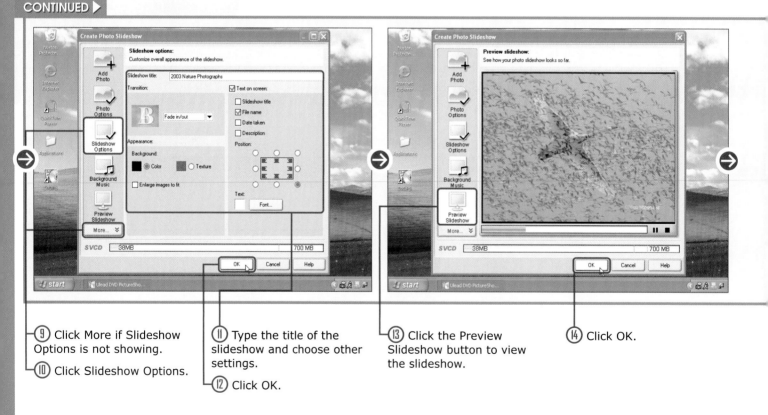

⑨ Click More if Slideshow Options is not showing.

⑩ Click Slideshow Options.

⑪ Type the title of the slideshow and choose other settings.

⑫ Click OK.

⑬ Click the Preview Slideshow button to view the slideshow.

⑭ Click OK.

Caution! ※

Older set-top DVD players may not be able to play either the VCD or SVCD discs. Some of the newer model set-top DVD players may have problems playing a CD-R disc but will play a CD-RW disc.

Did You Know? ※

When you create a video slideshow using Ulead DVD PictureShow 2, you can add digital video clips, music, and multiple slideshows. You can also create your own title screen with selectable menu options similar to those generally found in commercially produced DVD movies.

#97 CONTINUED

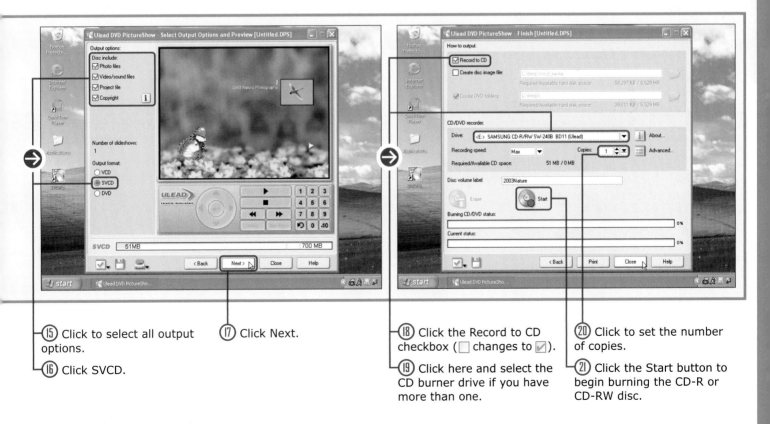

⑮ Click to select all output options.

⑯ Click SVCD.

⑰ Click Next.

⑱ Click the Record to CD checkbox (☐ changes to ☑).

⑲ Click here and select the CD burner drive if you have more than one.

⑳ Click to set the number of copies.

㉑ Click the Start button to begin burning the CD-R or CD-RW disc.

Create a
PHOTO CALENDAR

Everyone needs at least one calendar. Using Adobe Photoshop Album, you can easily create calendars that display your photography while providing 12 months' worth of calendar pages for keeping track of events. Creating a calendar is as easy as following the five steps in the Creations Wizard. You have a choice of six different styles, including styles for both horizontal and vertical pages, and you can display up to 13 photos, including one photo for the cover and one for each month. If you choose to add

captions below each photo you can do so by adding the desired captions to the image file.

Once you have created your photo calendar you can print it out on your own desktop photo printer or you can use one of the online services found in the Adobe Photoshop Album Calendar Creations Wizard. Photo calendars make excellent gifts. The next time you need to give a gift, make a photo calendar customized for the recipient using your photographs.

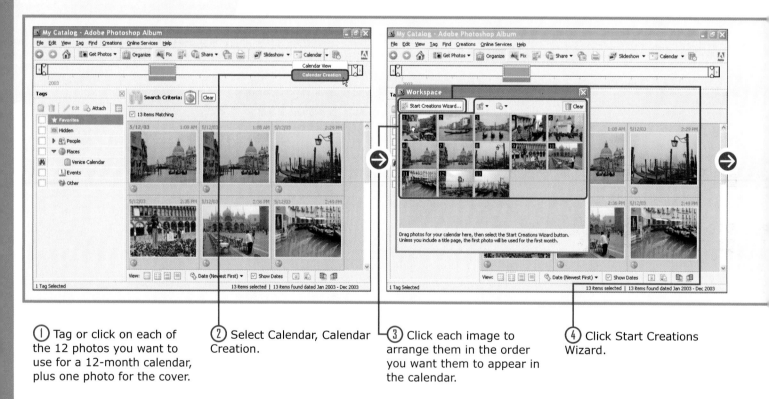

① Tag or click on each of the 12 photos you want to use for a 12-month calendar, plus one photo for the cover.

② Select Calendar, Calendar Creation.

③ Click each image to arrange them in the order you want them to appear in the calendar.

④ Click Start Creations Wizard.

#98

DIFFICULTY LEVEL

Did You Know? ✺

You can have photo captions printed below each photo. Place a check mark in the Include Captions box in Step 3 of the Calendar Creations Wizard and then enter captions in the digital photo files. To enter captions into the digital photo files using Adobe Photoshop Elements, click File⇨File Info to open the File Info dialog box, then type the caption in the Caption box and save the file.

Did You Know? ✺

If you do not have a copy of Adobe Photoshop Album and you want to make a photo calendar, you can download several Microsoft Word style sheets from the Microsoft Web site at officeupdate.Microsoft.com/templategallery. You can also download the Snapfish Photo Wizard at www.snapfish.com/photowizard and use the wizard to order prints online from Snapfish. Shutterfly (www.shutterfly.com) also offers a service for printing photo calendars.

CONTINUED ▶

─⑤ Click the calendar style you want.

─O You can drag the scroll bar downward to view all of the calendar styles.

O This area shows a preview of the selected calendar style.

─⑥ Click Next.

─⑦ If you want a title page, place a check mark next to the Title box and type the title.

─⑧ Click here and select a starting month and year.

⑨ Click here and select an ending month and year.

─⑩ Click Next.

Create a
PHOTO CALENDAR

Adobe Photoshop Album enables you to create a wide variety of photo-based print projects. In addition to creating calendars, you can make greeting cards, photo albums, and much more with a simple click of a button. Adobe Photoshop Album also lets you retouch photos, crop, and resize photos. This relatively low-priced software even provides tools for sharing your favorite photos with friends and loved ones online, including built-in templates for creating a Web photo gallery.

You do not have to use Adobe Photoshop Album to create your own photo calendars. Most imaging software vendors sell similar software, including Ulead Photo Explorer, Broderbund Calendar Creator, Microsoft Picture It!, and others. The market offers programs that are as basic or as sophisticated as your particular needs. So now that you have taken, enhanced, and archived wonderful digital photos, you can invest in a calendar application and share them in a way that is not only fun, but very practical.

CONTINUED ▶

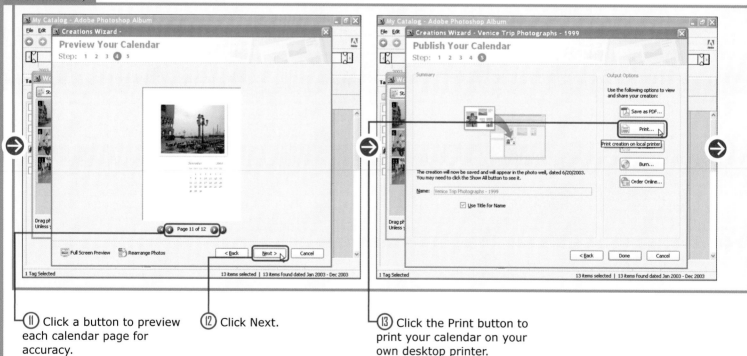

⑪ Click a button to preview each calendar page for accuracy.

⑫ Click Next.

⑬ Click the Print button to print your calendar on your own desktop printer.

Did You Know? ✳

You can create a PDF file instead of printing the calendar to your own desktop printer. After clicking the Save as PDF button, you can select settings to optimize the file for viewing onscreen, for printing, or for full resolution. This is a nice feature if you want to create a calendar and add dates to it using Adobe Acrobat and share the calendar with others. If you use the Optimize for Printing setting, you can add dates and then provide the file on a CD to others so that they can print out their own calendar with the high-resolution images. Or, you can create a 2.5MB file that is optimized for viewing onscreen and can be downloaded from a Web page.

98

CONTINUED

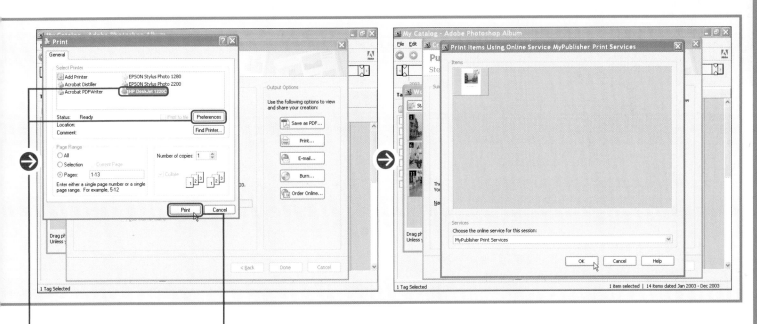

(14) Click the printer you want to use.

O Click here to choose any additional settings that are appropriate for your printer.

(15) Click Print to begin printing.

O You can also choose to use one of the online printing services by clicking Order Online in step **13** and using the Creations Wizard.

Create a
PHOTO
GREETING CARD

The next time you need a greeting card, you can make your own personalized card especially for the recipient using one or more of your photos. As you work through each step of the Greeting Card Creations Wizard, your steps are automatically saved in a file so that you can quickly make another copy or modify an existing card to create a new one.

One of the strengths of Adobe Photoshop Album is that the product is designed so that you can download new templates or styles for many of the Photo Creations when they become available. You can also use various online services such as MyPublisher Print Services and Shutterfly. After you have signed up for one of these services, you can use them as quickly as you can complete your digital photo projects. To see if new services are available, select Online Services, Check for New Services. If new services are available, they will be integrated into the Adobe Photoshop Album.

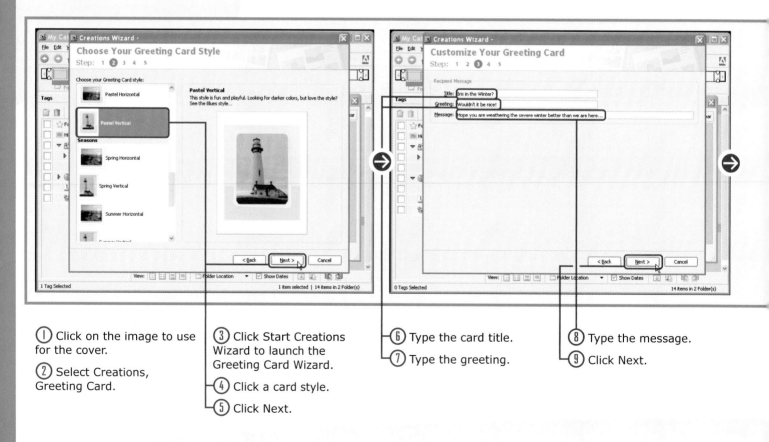

① Click on the image to use for the cover.

② Select Creations, Greeting Card.

③ Click Start Creations Wizard to launch the Greeting Card Wizard.

④ Click a card style.

⑤ Click Next.

⑥ Type the card title.

⑦ Type the greeting.

⑧ Type the message.

⑨ Click Next.

Did You Know? ※

Adobe Photoshop Album's greeting card makes it easy for you to print greeting cards with your own desktop printer. You can also publish cards as a PDF file or as an attachment for e-mail, plus you can save the card to a CD-ROM or order the card to be printed professionally from an online service vendor.

#99

DIFFICULTY LEVEL

Did You Know? ※

Many stationery vendors make greeting card paper and matching envelopes especially for use with inkjet printers. You can find tinted, glossy, embossed, matte, and many other varieties in a pre-scored format for easy and accurate folding. Check your local office supply store or order online from www.staples.com or www.officedepot.com.

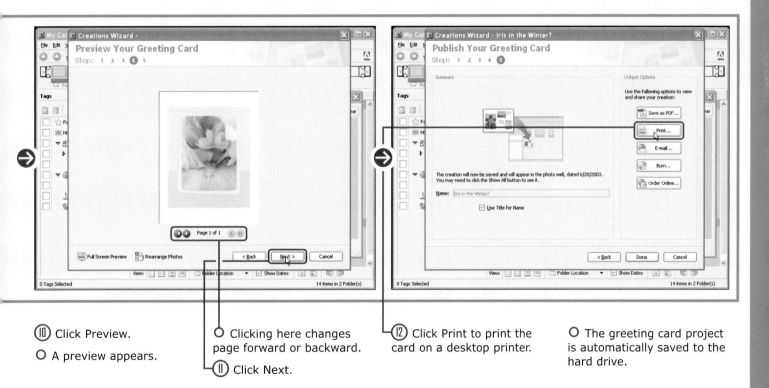

⑩ Click Preview.

○ A preview appears.

○ Clicking here changes page forward or backward.

⑪ Click Next.

⑫ Click Print to print the card on a desktop printer.

○ The greeting card project is automatically saved to the hard drive.

Create a
PHOTO MONTAGE

A popular thing to do with printed photographs is to cut them up and creatively place and glue them on a single board making a photo collage. The collage technique is good for assembling a group of photos taken on a vacation, a family get-together, or a sporting event. However, the process of creating a collage in this manner takes some skill and lots of time.

In sharp contrast, making a photo montage with Adobe Photoshop Elements is both easy and fun. Not only are all the photos printed on a single page (that

is why it is called a photo montage instead of a collage), but the process allows you to size and easily crop each image as needed.

Before you begin placing the digital photos on a new blank document, you should first roughly size the photos so that you minimize the work that it takes to resize them as you place them. When you have resized each photo, you can begin the simple process of dragging, dropping, placing, and sizing each digital photo.

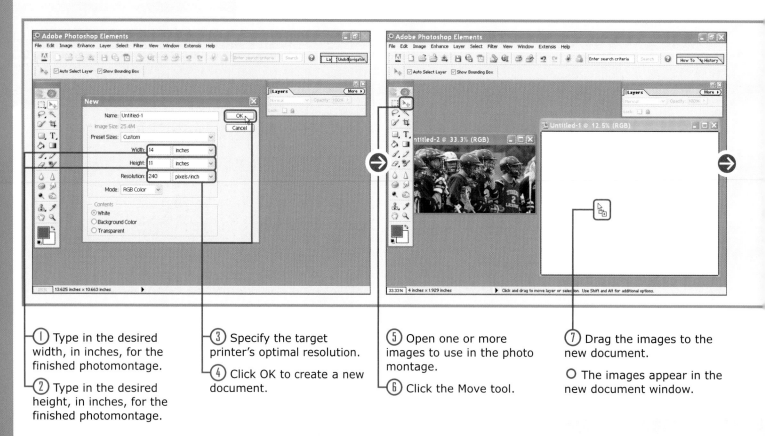

① Type in the desired width, in inches, for the finished photomontage.

② Type in the desired height, in inches, for the finished photomontage.

③ Specify the target printer's optimal resolution.

④ Click OK to create a new document.

⑤ Open one or more images to use in the photo montage.

⑥ Click the Move tool.

⑦ Drag the images to the new document.

O The images appear in the new document window.

#100

DIFFICULTY LEVEL

Did You Know? ※

When arranging photos in a photo montage, you can resize any image to fit the available space. Click an image to select it and then click and drag one of the handles to size the image. To maintain the image's aspect ratio, press Shift while adjusting the image size.

Did You Know? ※

When you have completed placing, sizing, and ordering all of the images in a photo montage, you can easily add a shadow line to each photo to add depth to your work. Simply click on each layer in the Layers palette and then click on your choice of shadow from the Drop Shadows styles found in the Layer Styles palette.

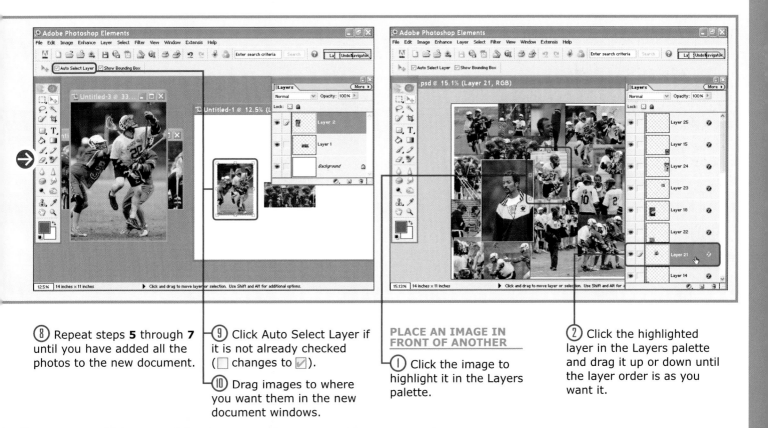

⑧ Repeat steps **5** through **7** until you have added all the photos to the new document.

⑨ Click Auto Select Layer if it is not already checked (☐ changes to ☑).

⑩ Drag images to where you want them in the new document windows.

PLACE AN IMAGE IN FRONT OF ANOTHER

① Click the image to highlight it in the Layers palette.

② Click the highlighted layer in the Layers palette and drag it up or down until the layer order is as you want it.

INDEX

INDEX

INDEX

INDEX